Introduction

God created us for a purpose-filled life.

How old must a child be before he/she can begin to understand his/her God-given purpose? Most of us can remember playing games as children about being, teachers, doctors, preachers, parents, actors, athletes and so on. Children are imaginative, adventurous, often fearless, and bold about discovering, "What I want to be when I grow up." So often, when children get older, they lose their focus and childlike zeal as the events of life take over the outcomes of life.

This book is so important, because it takes the concepts of Identity and Destiny, 7 Steps to a Purpose-Filled Life, and transforms it into an adventure story, complete with all of the assessments and exercises and it becomes a work that is understood by children. It is written to help children identify the skills and gifts that God has placed within them so that they might learn at a young age, and begin to direct their education, hobbies, and relationships in the direction that is most pleasing to God, and most fulfilling to them. Proverb 22:6 says that we are to train a child in the way he/she should go, and when they are older, they will not turn away from it. (*paraphrase.*) In the original language, it is emphasized that we are to train our children according to their individual inclination, or God-given bent. Parents are uniquely equipped to understand their children's passions, strengths and giftings. As children grow, their personalities begin to shine. This book is written to equip parents and children's ministers, coaches, and children's counselors; to discover the deep desires and strengths of children. It is best suited to 4th and 5th grade students, but 2nd and 3rd grade students are able to understand and gain insights from it as well.

Before you Begin.

This book was originally created as a Children's Church Curriculum and the series was presented in class with a group of students. Each lesson was used for a weekly class and it took 19 weeks to complete. Another way to work through the material could be a lesson a day for 19 days. The book is divided into 3 parts; The Intellectual Phase, The Bridge, or "What's Stopping You?" and The Spiritual Phase. These parts can be presented in a 4 week plan; dividing part 1 into two weeks, and devoting a week to each, part 2 and part 3. However you choose to present the class, the attention span of the student, and their level of engagement with the material will determine the effectiveness of the lessons. A journal page is provided with each lesson to teach the concept of journaling and to note the student's progress. This bound book offers a valuable tool to keep all of the assessments and journal pages for the student. I recommend each student have their own copy of the book. It becomes a treasury of information about the student allowing them to refer back to it for years to come. When students reach their mid-teens, I recommend they review the process using the book by Tom and Pam Wolf, Identity and Destiny, 7 Steps to a Purpose Filled Life.

Prior to teaching the series, in a classroom setting, meet with the parents so they know about the journey ahead for their boys and girls. An outline for this meeting is provided in the appendix.

There are object lessons, games, activities and journal pages provided for each lesson. When using the book in a one- on - one situation, the active games may not apply. It is possible to find some of the activities, such as The River Crossing activity in an online challenge.

At the end of the appendix there are four pages called My Mosaic. These pages summarize the work that the students did over the course of several weeks and provide a keepsake for future reference. You can fill in the blanks of the mosaic as you progress through the course, or you can complete it at the end of the course which serves as a review of all of the accomplishments of the past several weeks. The completion of the course is quite a milestone for children and a celebration of their achievement underscores the importance of the series. A party is a good way to finalize the lessons and each student can be presented with a certificate as a keepsake along with their completed book.

Acknowledgments

I am grateful to Tom and Pam Wolf from whom the inspiration and the original work, Identity and Destiny - 7 Steps to a Purpose-Filled Life have been adapted to suit the capacity and the imagination of children. With your help I am aspiring to "Be the Difference!"

To my pastors, Tim and Cindy Byler, I want to say a heart-felt, "Thank You!" For years of leadership, exhortation, and friendship. You have coached and pastored me through many pathways and I'm so glad our journey continues together!

To the parents of the 2nd - 5th Grade class at Connection Church, 2012- 2013, for allowing me the opportunity to "practice with purpose" with their sons and daughters. To the boys and girls of the class, I trust that the mosaic journal that we developed over the course of our study will remain an inspiration to you for years to come.

To Donna Ploth, my long-time friend, fellow member of Connection Church, Identity and Destiny Coach, and the proofreader for this work. Thank you for your tireless efforts and excellent advice. Your enthusiasm helped to spark creativity and the desire to plow through when I got "stuck." I loved it when you said, "What happens next? I can't wait to get the next chapter!" God bless you my friend.

To my family, now grown, who have allowed me the opportunity to pour countless hours for many years into study, teaching and writing. You have graciously allowed me to pursue my passion and have never complained. God bless you for that!

Especially to my husband, best friend, and co-laborer in children's ministry and in life. Thank you for always affirming me and encouraging me to keep forging ahead. For hours, days, and months of helping me plow through the details, and 37 years of working and growing together.

I give credit and thanks to the Lord as my personal motivator for inspiration, opportunities to serve and relate to children, and the grace to continue daily in a relationship with Him that exceeds all of my dreams and expectations.

IDENTITY AND DESTINY
AMAZING KIDS FOR

Contents
Part 1 - The Intellectual Phase

IDENTITY AND DESTINY
AMAZING KIDS FOR

Contents

IDENTITY AND DESTINY
AMAZING KIDS FOR

Contents

IDENTITY AND DESTINY
AMAZING KIDS *FOR*

Contents

Identity and Destiny

Part 3 - The Spiritual Phase

You do the Steps - and God does the Rest!

IDENTITY AND DESTINY
AMAZING KIDS FOR

Lesson 1

Memory Verse: JEREMIAH 29:11 For I know the plans I have for you," says the Lord. "They are plans for good and not for disaster, to give you a future and a hope.
Objective: To discover your true life purpose; only 3% of people ever do.

⇨**Introduction:**
You are about to enter in to an adventure with Chris and Zoé and along with them you will learn:
* God loves you and has a plan for your life.
*You are one-of-a-kind and uniquely designed to fulfill your purpose.
*You will never be truly satisfied until you find that purpose.
*The plans and purpose God has for your life matter - both here and in eternity.
*God wants to touch your life and use you in ways you can only imagine.

So let's begin our story.
Chris Kingson lived in a suburb with rows and rows of houses. Nicely manicured yards, fenced in back yards with pools and swing sets, and a great big field at the end of the street where a lot of kids gathered after school to play ball or ride bikes.
On this particular beautiful summer afternoon Chris wanted to enjoy a bike ride to his best friend's house. "Hey Mom! Can I go to Zoé's for a while?" He shouted "May I?" Was the muted reply from the kitchen. "Oh Yeah," Chris corrected himself, "May I go to Zoé's?" "Sure Chris but don't be late for dinner," Mom replied, "We're having lasagna." "Woo Hoo! My favorite, I won't be late!" Mom laughed as Chris ran out the door with his dog Bernie at his heels.

Zoé lived a couple of blocks away, where the sidewalks and streetlights ended and the road turned to dirt and gravel. Her parents owned a farm on several acres and Chris loved to visit the woods, the animals and Zoé's large family. Chris especially loved the tree house that Zoé's Dad and brothers built.

MOSAIC PIECE

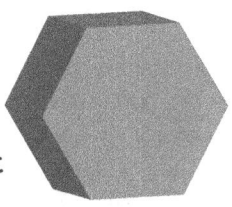

PURPOSE: something set up as an object or result to be achieved

It was filled with treasure accumulated over several years, like favorite ball gloves, old coins in a jar, old signs nailed to the wall, flash lights for camp - outs, and trinkets galore. Arrow heads and shiny stones lined a shelf on the wall and Chris loved to add to the collection whenever he found something worthy of a special spot on the shelf. Today Chris had a shiny piece of blue glass to contribute.
As usual, Bernie barked loudly as he saw the drive leading to the farm house. The screen door slammed as Zoé ran out to meet her friends. She bounded down the front steps two at a time and headed straight for the tree house out back. "Caw, caw!" suddenly greeted the friends as Perry, Zoé's pet falcon swooped down to join the fun. Chris hopped off his bike and parked it at the base of the tree and Bernie sniffed around as if to see who else had visited their special spot. The friends climbed up the boards that formed a ladder and Perry perched in the branches of the tree. As he climbed into the treehouse, Chris pulled out his shiny piece of glass, he held it up for Zoé to see, "Here you see an amazing, magical, piece of blue glass!" He declared. Zoé laughed, "Magical?" "Sure, look at this," Chris held the blue treasure up to catch the sun's rays and the colors of the rainbow reflected from it in beams that glowed on the treehouse floor and walls. "Oh, that's beautiful," Zoé expressed admiration for the piece confirming that Chris truly had a treasure to add to the collection on the shelf. He placed it carefully beside several old glass bottles and pulled down a deck of cards, "Care to get beat in a game today?" He joked. "We'll see about that!" Zoé was ready for the challenge.

Lesson 1 page 2

The friends lost track of time, as their game stretched out into the entire afternoon. A shadow crossed the floor and they didn't notice. Bernie whined and Perry cawed, and still the friends played and laughed and heard nothing. Suddenly, as if out of nowhere, a large clap of thunder boomed and a bolt of lightning flashed nearby. "Yikes! That was close!" Chris was startled and was now looking out the window at the storm that had blown in. "Where did that come from?" Zoé wondered. The tree began to sway as the rain started to pour down hard. The kids knew that trees are dangerous places in a lightning storm, so one after the other, they began to climb down the slippery ladder. "BOOM, CRASH!" The thunder and lightning lit the sky and shook the ground and then Chris felt himself falling, and falling. His arms and legs churned like windmills as he frantically tried to grab the ladder and then THUD! Nothing.

Chris opened his eyes and rubbed his head, "OW! What happened?" The sun glittered on his face so brightly that he closed his eyes and turned his head away to adjust. He sat up with a groan. He seemed fine except a bump on the head. "Wow Chris, are you okay?" Zoé seemed worried about him and Bernie was right there whining and rubbing his head against Chris's leg. "Hey Bernie, I guess you woke me up huh boy?" Chris patted his pet's head and noticed Bernie had something in his mouth. "What's this?" Chris took what looked like a scroll of paper from Bernie's mouth. "Wow, look at this, it looks like a map or something." The friends studied the scroll more closely and read at the bottom,

Two roads diverged in a wood, and I took the one less traveled and that has made all of the difference. R. Frost.

"This looks like a clue or something." Zoé stroked her chin as she thought about what it could mean. Zoé helped Chris to his feet and they noticed a sign post at the edge of the woods, and a crossroad that they had not seen before. It had two arrows that pointed at very similar paths; one leading left and the other right. The path to the right was worn and tracked with footprints while the path on the left appeared perfectly smooth.

"We need to take the path to the left to see what this is all about," Chris was ready for an adventure as always, and Zoé was not about to be left out.

* * * * *

Have you ever wondered, 'Who am I, why am I here?' Most people ask these questions at one time or another. Maybe you haven't because you already know: **YOU ARE A CHILD OF GOD!**
There are some things about us that are common to all people:

> We are planned by God.
> We are part of His family.
> We are created to be like Jesus.
> We are shaped to serve God.
> We are made for a mission.

But we are also individuals and within God's plan for us all, each one of us has a unique purpose. God has given each of us special gifts, talents and abilities and He wants to help us figure out His specific plan for our life.

⇨ **OBJECT LESSON: Create a Picture of How God Created You**
You will need paper, crayons, colored pencils or markers and several shapes of various types made from card stock or cookie cutters or anything that the students can trace onto a sheet of paper. Use geometric shapes, fruits, sports, dance shoes, objects like houses, trees, animals, people, or anything you like.
Ask the class to pick the items that tell something about themselves. Ask them to use color to help describe their choices. They can write on their shapes to help describe them too.
 Ask volunteers to share their pictures with the class. Your artwork tells alot about God's unique design for you.

⇨**Object Talk: Why Snow?**
You'll need shaved ice for a demonstration. (This can also double as a great snack. Snowballs with flavored syrup.)

Proverbs 16:4 (NLT)
The Lord has made everything for his own purposes.

God says He made everything for a purpose. So what purpose do you think snow has in His plan? It's beautiful, fun to play in, you can make snowmen, forts and snowballs with it!
Have any of you ever played in snow? If so, what was that like? What did you do with the snow? What happens the minute it gets warm outside? The snow melts away and becomes a puddle.

Sprinkle some shaved ice on the table top and let the class watch as it melts.

What purpose does the snow serve now?
Snow is actually frozen water. In cold climates, it keeps animals and people from being thirsty. Snow is frozen rain and we know that we need rain to keep the earth hydrated.

Even when things seem to last for a short time, like snow, it has a specific purpose and is important in God's plan. If snow is that important, how much value do you suppose your own life has in the eyes of God?

Here's another fun fact about snow.
Did you know that every snow flake is unique? Under a microscope, you can see that every snowflake looks slightly different. Even something as temporary as snow that melts is so important to God that He took the time to craft each one differently. We are like snowflakes in that each of us is unique. We all have different gifts, talents and abilities. We are all part of God's family yet each one of us is one of a kind.

⇨**Active Learning: Tricky Bear Game**
You will need a plastic cup for each player in the game. Also the "Tricky Bear Song" can be found on the internet.
Seat all of the players in a circle and play the tricky bear song for them a couple of times until they pick it up. Then ask the students to try to play the game and sing the song themselves. Watch out, there's a tricky part!
Allow the class to play the game a few times, then ask, "Do you see how we all work together to make this game successful?"
"What happens when one person makes a mistake? We all have to stop the game and start over. As different as we are, we must remember that each of us plays an important role God's plan."
"What happens when we successfully make it through the whole song? WE CELEBRATE and CHEER!

IDENTITY AND DESTINY FOR AMAZING KIDS

Lesson 1

NAME: _____ DATE: _____

MEMORY VERSE: *JEREMIAH 29:11 For I know the plans I have for you," says the Lord. "They are plans for good and not for disaster, to give you a future and a hope.*

*Write the verse here
memorize it at home*

Objective: To discover your true life's purpose.

MOSAIC PIECE

PURPOSE: something set up as an object or result to be achieved.

> Two roads diverged in a wood, and I took the one less traveled and that has made all of the difference.

THE 1st CLUE: A LINE ADAPTED FROM THE POEM BY ROBERT FROST, "THE ROAD NOT TRAVELED."

MY BIG AHA!
What does the clue above mean? Why do you think one choice makes all the difference? Chris and Zoé are about to become part of the 3% who find their purpose. Will you?

IDENTITY AND DESTINY
AMAZING KIDS FOR

Lesson 2

Bible Lesson: Haggai Inspires Israel
Memory Verse: John 10:10 My purpose is to give them a rich and satisfying life.
Objective: Begin to Discover Your Purpose

⇨**Meet Coach Tom:**

Chris and Zoé began their walk on the path that bore to the left. They discovered that the path was soft sand, like the beach sand that the water never reaches. It was soft and hard to walk in. "I wonder why no one ever goes this way," Zoé questioned. "Oops," She laughed as her foot slipped in the fluffy deep sand. "I guess because this isn't easy to do. Maybe we should turn around and take the other path like everyone else did." Chris shook his head, "Not if we want to figure out where our clue is leading us." Zoé trudged on lifting her feet high and nodded her agreement, "You're right, we need to find out what the clue is leading us to." The friends began to chat about what type of treasure they might discover. They recalled every pirate movie they had ever seen, every story about lost cities filled with gold, and every adventure tale they could think of, as they trudged along the soft, sandy path. "Wow, I'm getting tired," Chris wiped his forehead with the back of his arm. "I wonder how much longer we have to walk." Chris shielded his eyes from the sun as he tried to find Zoé's falcon. "I wish we could see what's ahead from Perry's point of view." Zoé called to her pet, "What do you see from up there girl?" Perry swooped down and cawed. Chris laughed as if he understood Perry. "Yes, it's just as she said," He turned to see Bernie who looked funny as he trudged over the sandy mounds that were left by their footprints. "What did she say boy?" "Woof, woof!" was Bernie's interpretation. The friends laughed and continued on still determined to see what was ahead.

MOSAIC PIECE

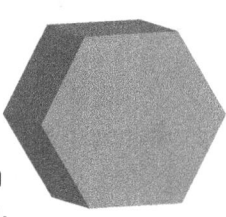

DESTINY: It's what you do just by being you.

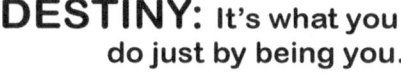

Suddenly the friends heard a shrill whistle, "TWEET, TWEET!" Came the sound from somewhere just ahead. "I heard you coming from a mile away," greeted them next as they rounded a bend and saw a man standing before them. He carried a clipboard, wore a coaches uniform and ball cap and a whistle around his neck that obviously produced the call they heard. "Hi, I'm Coach Tom, and who are you?" The children introduced themselves and their pets, and explained the clue that brought them on this journey. "Ah, I see, so we have some adventurers on a great quest, huh?" Coach Tom nodded toward a stream that flowed beside the path a short way ahead, "I bet you could use a break and some more direction." "Yes sir!" The friends agreed, and Coach Tom encouraged them to get a drink and sit awhile so that he could give them some more information for their journey.

As the friends settled on some soft grass to rest, Coach said, "You're the first people to come this way in a very long time." The children seemed surprised, "Why is that?" They wondered, "Aren't other people curious to see where their clues lead them?" Coach Tom sighed, "Most people don't have a clue because they don't take the time to look for one. They hustle about, heading who knows where, but in a big hurry to get there." Then he perked up, "So you want to see where your clue is leading you?" "We sure do!" The friends agreed. "Alright then, first tell me, where you are." Coach asked this question and the friends looked around and shrugged, "We aren't exactly sure where we are." "Right! Then here's what's next," pulling out his clipboard, the Coach was ready to begin.

Coach Tom's clipboard: The Purpose Scorecard

Answer the following questions using this scale:
1 never true, 2 rarely true, 3 sometimes true,
4 often true, 5 always true. Circle the number that best describes you.
(For younger students, read the statements aloud and help them see where to place their score.)

1 I wake up in the morning energized and ready for the day.
1 2 3 4 5

2 I love my life and enjoy what I do.
1 2 3 4 5

3 I feel good about my life and the choices that I make.
1 2 3 4 5

4 I love God and I've asked Jesus to be my Savior.
1 2 3 4 5

5 I know my gifts and strengths and I use them in what I do each day.
1 2 3 4 5

6 I am very clear about what I value and what I believe.
1 2 3 4 5

7 I live my life according to my values and beliefs.
1 2 3 4 5

8 I know my unique gifts, talents, and experiences that make me who I am.
1 2 3 4 5

9 I know the things that I love the most in my life.
1 2 3 4 5

10 I know what is most important in my life.
1 2 3 4 5

11 I live my life according to what I know is most important.
1 2 3 4 5

12 My life is balanced in a healthy way between my friends, my family, having fun, other activities, chores and school.
1 2 3 4 5

13 I know God has a purpose for my life and I know what it is.
1 2 3 4 5

14 I live my life according to God's purpose for me every day.
1 2 3 4 5

15 I can easily tell others about my purpose.
1 2 3 4 5

16 I think about my purpose often. I take time to think about where I am, and where I want to be.
1 2 3 4 5

17 I know how to move in the direction of my purpose.
1 2 3 4 5

18 I know how to pray and think to discover my deepest desires.
1 2 3 4 5

19 I am not afraid or frustrated about life.
1 2 3 4 5

20 I have the freedom to do what I love and I have fun doing it.
1 2 3 4 5

Now add up the total of all of the answers that you chose.
Write the total here: _____

If you scored 85 - 100 Congratulations!
You're well on your way to a life of satisfaction, confidence and peace. Look at all the areas that you scored less than 5 and focus on improving in those areas.

If you scored 70 - 84
Your life is good. You do have understanding about your purpose but you could use some help to go from good to great! Focus on the areas where you need to improve, especially prayer and reading your Bible.

If you scored 50 - 69
You probably feel like you're doing okay compared to other people, but you're not certain about your purpose and you may feel like life is more work than fun. Life is more fun when we live according to God's priorities for us.

If you scored 30 - 49
Life could be better. Try to step back and take some time to pray, look at your life, and consider what you can do differently to plan your work and fun activities according to God's plan for you.

If you scored less than 30
Life just seems to happen to you. You don't have direction and you may feel tired all the time. You have the tools in your hand now to find your purpose, gifts and talents.

Lesson 2 page 3

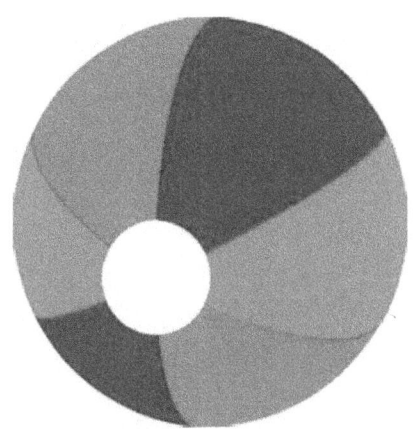

⇨ **Seven Steps to Purpose**

Over the next several weeks we are going to take a journey along with our friends Chris and Zoé as we discover our purpose.
We will continue to find clues, experience adventure, and discover pieces to our mosaic. Let's follow the map that is being laid out for us and when we are finished you will have your own personal Identity and Destiny statements.

You do the steps - and God will do the rest!

John 10:10 My purpose is to give them a rich and satisfying life.

It's in the Book!

In the Bible there is a story about a prophet named Haggai who lived about 500 years before Jesus was born. He challenged the Jews to rebuild God's temple in Jerusalem because it had been destroyed by invading armies. The people were more concerned with building homes for themselves and making clothes and growing food, but it seemed like they were never satisfied. It was as if their wallets had holes in them, and every time they made some money, a lot of it fell through the hole and got lost.
Haggai helped the people see that they had lost their focus. When they first moved back into Jerusalem, God told them to rebuild the temple. They got busy with survival and forgot to obey His orders.
Haggai had a solution for them. Rebuild the temple - the place where people gather to worship God. When the people obeyed God, the blessings began to flow.

Make God first in your life and He will take care of everything else.

⇨ **Active Learning: Dodge Ball**

You will need one or two beach balls and an open space large enough for the group to run. Set up your boundaries and divide the class into two equal groups. Place a tape line on the floor in the center of the playing area and mark boundaries for the back and sides of each side of the playing area. Put the beach ball on the center line and explain the rules. Players must try to retrieve the ball and hit an opponent with it without crossing the line. If the players cross a boundary they are out. If the opponent catches the ball they are safe and can return fire, but the thrower is out. If a player is hit by the ball they must sit out. The team that is eliminated first loses the match.
Two balls in play at once will make the game more lively. Play best two out of three rounds or as time allows.

At the end of the game ask the players:
How did it feel to be tagged out and have to sit on the sidelines?
How did it feel to be in the game and firing the ball at someone?

Think about this:
God wants all of us to be on His team and play our part. When we find our purpose, we become the best players we can be.
When you have purpose you have energy, confidence, focus and fun!

God wants your life to be successful!

IDENTITY AND DESTINY
AMAZING KIDS FOR

Lesson 2

NAME: _____ DATE: _____

MEMORY VERSE: *John 10:10*
My purpose is to give them a rich and satisfying life.
Write the verse here.
Memorize it at home.

Objective: Begin to Discover Your Purpose Mosaic

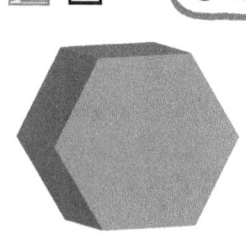

MOSAIC PIECE
DESTINY: It's what you do just by being you.

CAPTURE IT!
How did you score on the Purpose Scorecard by
Coach Tom? _____

Did your score surprise you?
Why, or why not?

You are here.

MY BIG AHA!
What action step can you take right now to start seeing improvement on your purpose scorecard? Based on our memory verse
today, what do you think God says is His purpose? How can you
have this kind of life?

IDENTITY AND DESTINY
AMAZING KIDS FOR

Lesson 3

Bible Lesson:
Memory Verse: 1 Thessalonians 1:4 (TM) It is clear to us, friends, that God not only loves you very much but also has put his hand on you for something special.
Objective: How are You Wired?

 **Will You Get in the Game?**

Chris and Zoé completed their score cards given them by Coach Tom. They added up all of the numbers for one final score and Coach Tom congratulated them, "Well done! You are both on your way to discovering your purpose! There are a few areas that you can develop more and this score card will be handy in the future, so hold on to it." Then Coach Tom gave each of them a glass tile that sparkled in the sun. "You'll want to keep these in a safe place too, they are a piece of your mosaic and they represent the good work you did today." Chris and Zoé carefully placed their tiles in a zipper pocket so that they wouldn't lose them, "Thanks Coach Tom!" They glowed with their accomplishment and the encouragement that they received. "Are we going to build a mosaic?" Zoé asked. "You sure are, and you've already begun," smiled the coach. "Think of it like a treasure hunt, are you ready for the next piece of the mosaic?" "Yes sir!" the kids agreed. Bernie barked at all of the excitement while Perry circled above them looking around for a snack.

Coach Tom led Chris and Zoé to a field where it looked like a game was underway. "How would you like to get into the game?" Coach asked. Being very competitive both kids agreed, "Sure, it looks like fun!" "Good," Coach began to explain, "This is a game of Who Am I Dodge Ball." The kids looked puzzled and Coach continued to explain, "The game is played just like Dodge Ball, but notice the back of the jerseys that the players are wearing."

MOSAIC PIECE

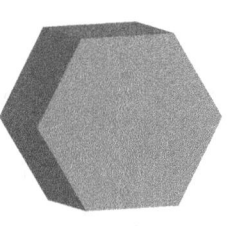

IDENTITY: It's who I am - not what I do.

Chris read out loud, "One and Only." "Wonderfully Made." and "God Loves Me." Zoé read, "Unique." and "Made for a Purpose." There were several more players with jerseys that had similar sayings on their back. Chris wondered out loud, "Are those the names of the players?" "Yes, the names say a lot about the person, now it's your turn," Coach pulled a jersey for each of them out of a large duffle bag beside the sideline bench. Chris got a jersey that said, "Christ Bearer," while Zoé wore one that said, "God Life." The kids loved the names on their shirts and they were anxious to begin the game. A few players sat on the bench watching the action. They had been tagged out and were waiting for an opportunity to get back in the game. Coach Tom blew his whistle, "TWEET, TWEET!" All the players stopped and looked to him for his direction. "Folks, two new players are entering the game, let's give it your all!" Chris and Zoé ran onto the field and took their positions and at the sound of the whistle the game began. Bernie ran up and down the sideline barking at all of the action, he was excited too.

The players worked well together and the competition was tough, but one by one the players were eliminated from the game and sat on the bench to rest and drink some water. After a very exciting match with Zoé's team being the winner, all of the players gathered around Coach Tom to take a break. "Now that you're in the game can anyone tell me what you've learned?" Coach asked. "A player wearing a jersey that said, "Chosen" spoke up. "I learned that we have to work together to win the game." Several heads nodded.

A player from the winning team offered, "I learned that we do our best when we all do our part." A round of High 5's and "Way to go," circulated among the team. "Great observations," Coach Tom agreed. "Remember this, if you want to hear God say, "Well done," when you meet Him face to face one day, you must understand that He has created only one you and He has a very specific purpose that only you can fufill." The players all nodded thoughtfully. Each one considering his or her specific role both on the team as a player as well as in the bigger game of life.

Coach Tom continued, "There are Seven Steps to Purpose, and you are all well on your way to the next step. Each of you have earned a piece of your mosaic, at this point and I'll give each of you a clue to the next step on your journey. The players were all rested and ready for the next clue. Coach passed out scrolls to every player and one by one, they read their clue and started off. Chris noticed that the players started off in several directions, usually in pairs. He looked up as Coach Tom smiled down at him and handed him a scroll. He unrolled it and read it.

> "If any of you lacks wisdom, he should ask God who gives generously to all without finding fault." James 1:5

Chris showed Zoé his clue and they laughed because her's was the same. "I think we'd better pray and ask God which way we're supposed to go next." The kids agreed and did just that. Just as they said, "Amen," they heard the familiar, "Caw, caw," that meant that Perry spotted something. Chris and Zoé jumped to their feet and started to follow the clever hunting bird.

⇨ **OBJECT LESSON: Your Personality Style**

Give each student 4 different colored highlighters. Assign each column its own color such as blue for column A, orange for column B, green for column C, and yellow for column D.
This will make the scoring process much easier for children. Younger students will need a helper as they mark their score sheets and add the results.

Use the journal page to record the results of the student's score card.

Active Game:

After working on their score cards the class will need to stretch their legs. Give them an opportunity to play another game of "Who Am I" Dodge Ball.

This time, ask the students if they have a better idea of the name they will wear on their jersey.

Lesson 3 page 3

⇨ DISC: THE LANGUAGE OF BEHAVIOR

Harvard Psychologist William Moulton Marston developed a theory that describes 4 classic styles of human behavior. It's called the DISC profile.

D = Dominant, Driving Personality
I = Influencing and Inspiring
S = Steady and Stable
C = Correct and Compliant

The profile will help you discover how you are "wired" to behave; how you communicate and interact with others, and how you make decisions.

Step 1 On each of the 24 rows, two options are offered. For each of the 24 rows, highlight the option that BEST describes your preferred work style.

	A	B	C	D
1	Collect ideas and solutions and study them carefully	Find creative solutions and tell others about your favorites		
2		Find creative solutions and tell others about your favorites	Make decisions and don't change your mind	
3			Make decisions and don't change your mind	Find out what others think before you decide
4	Collect ideas and solutions and study them carefully		Make decisions and don't change your mind	
5		Find creative solutions and tell others about your favorites		Find out what others think before you decide
6	Collect ideas and solutions and study them carefully			Find out what others think before you decide
7	Think of others and follow the rules	Fun and cheerful		
8		Fun and cheerful	Self-confident, ask a lot of questions	
9			Self-confident, ask a lot of questions	Dependable, warm, friendly, like things as they are
10	Think of others and follow the rules		Self-confident, ask a lot of questions	
11		Fun and cheerful		Dependable, warm, friendly, like things as they are
12	Think of others and follow the rules			Dependable, warm, friendly, like things as they are
13	Neat, organized and like things done right	Convincing and encouraging		
14		Convincing and encouraging	Straight to the point and want to win	
15			Straight to the point and want to win	Patient and steady
16	Neat, organized and like things done right		Straight to the point and want to win	
17		Convincing and encouraging		Patient and steady
18	Neat, organized and like things done right			Patient and steady
19	Look for exact answers	Popular and well-known by others		
20		Popular and well-known by others	You get things done	
21			You get things done	Dependable and stable
22	Look for exact answers		You get things done	
23		Popular and well-known by others		Patient and steady
24	Look for exact answers			Patient and steady
TOTAL				

Step 2 Score the quiz by counting the number of answers you highlighted in each column and write the totals in the boxes at the bottom of the quiz.

IDENTITY AND DESTINY
AMAZING KIDS FOR
Lesson 3

NAME: _____ DATE: _____

MEMORY VERSE: *1 Thessalonians 1:4 (TM) It is clear to us, friends, that God not only loves you very much but also has put his hand on you for something special.*

Write the verse here. Memorize it at home.

_____

_____

_____

_____

MY BIG AHA!
What action step can you take right now to start seeing improvement on your purpose scorecard? Based on our memory verse today, what do you think God says is His purpose? How can you have this kind of life?

MOSAIC PIECE
IDENTITY:
It's who I am - not what I do.

CAPTURE IT!
Use the totals from each column on your worksheet from the DISC quiz and let's translate them.

Your **D** is the score in the **C** box - write it here: _____

Your **I** is the score in the **B** box - write it here: _____

Your **S** is the score in the **D** box - write it here: _____

Your **C** is the score in the **A** box - write it here: _____

In which area do you have the highest number? _____

Which area is the second highest? _____

These are clues to your personality style. It's a key ingredient to the unique design that God made when He formed you.

IDENTITY AND DESTINY
AMAZING KIDS FOR

Lesson 4

Bible Lesson:
Memory Verse: Romans 12:4-5 Just as our bodies have many parts and each part has a special function, so it is with Christ's body. We are many parts of one body, and we all belong to each other.

Objective: To Find Out How You are Wired

⇨ **Team Work.**

Chris, Zoé and Bernie headed toward the direction that Perry was flying. Every now and then, Perry would swoop down and land on Zoé's arm as if to be sure that the friends were still following her. Straight ahead there was a small hill and Perry flew toward it. Bernie barked and ran as if he had picked up a new scent. Chris and Zoé picked up their pace and soon reached the top of the hill. On the other side, at the base of the hill, a group of people were gathered beside a wide river and seemed deep in conversation. As Bernie barked and ran toward them, they all looked up and saw Chris and Zoé approaching. "Oh good!!" A boy who was taller than Chris and had skin like dark chocolate, greeted them, "We can use your help." Zoé recognized the boy as one of the players from her dodge ball team. "Hi," she laughed, "I'm Zoé, why do you need our help?" The boy stretched out his hand in greeting, "I remember you and your lightning speed on the ball field. My name is Leon. We're trying to figure out how to get across this river," he pointed in the direction of the water that looked like iced tea. It was brown but very clear.

The rest of the group joined in the introductions, "I'm Reese," the pretty girl who greeted them looked like a cheerleader. She had a long blonde pony tail that bounced and swayed everytime she moved.
Her greeting was so bubbly you could almost hear her smile with every word she spoke. "And I'm Grace," smiled a more soft spoken yet warm and friendly girl. Her jet black hair and almond eyes shone beautifully in the sun and revealed her Asian heritage.

MOSAIC PIECE
ASSIGNMENT: What God is asking you to do next.

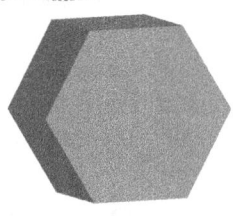

"Over there is Brodie,"
Leon pointed with his thumb to a boy with red hair, freckled nose and big round glasses, who stood still by the river bank studying the situation. He was so deep in thought that he hardly noticed the new arrivals.
"Hey everybody it's nice to meet you, I'm Chris, this is my pal Bernie, and Perry is the one who helped us find you," he pointed skyward as he made his introductions. Perry soared above them and the new friends were very impressed. Perry and Bernie were expert trackers and they made a great addition to the party of adventurers.

Now that the introductions were made, Leon returned to addressing Zoé's question. "We all got clues that led us this far and now we are trying to figure out what to do next." Reese added cheerfully, "With all of us working together, I'm sure we'll figure something out." Grace added, "Brodie has been studying the situation for sometime now." Then she called out, "Hey Brodie, do you have any ideas yet?" Brodie finally turned to look at the others and sqinted as the sun hit his glasses, "By the looks of it, this river is very deep. It's hard to tell because the water is so clear you can see the bottom, but I'm sure we would have to swim." "Wow!" Chris rubbed his forehead as he considered that idea. "The river is pretty wide too, I'm not sure if we could make it all the way across." Brodie had even considered the woods nearby, and wondered if they could build a bridge with tree limbs, but he quickly dismissed that idea too.

Zoé had a thought that caused her to laugh out loud. "What's so funny?" The others wanted to know. "Do any of you know the song about going on a bear hunt?" She asked. Several heads nodded but the new friends looked a little confused. "In the song," Zoé continued, "You sing about several ways to continue your journey. Since we we can't go over it, and we can't go through it, why don't we try to go around the river?" Chris was skeptical, "Around a river? How far do you think we'll have to go to do that?" Zoé replied, "Well, I don't know, but since we know we can't do the first two options, going around seems the only likely solution." Brodie nodded thoughtfully, "Why don't we head to the line of trees? They seem to merge on the river not too far from here." He pointed to the trees as he spoke. Since this seemed to be the only logical option, the friends agreed and started to move in that direction. As they walked, the friends chatted and laughed, told stories about themselves and got to know one another better.

⇨Active Learning: The Bear Hunt Song

(If you aren't familiar with this song search online to learn the words and tune.)
Create an adventure by singing the song with your class. Do the motions that are recommended for each of the steps in the song. Running through the grass, swimming across a river, climbing up a hill. Use as many as you like. (*In our class, I led the students to a dark, empty class room and I called it a cave. As I entered the room I turned and shouted, "BEAR!" The girls all screamed and turned to run. The boys ran then tried to act brave. You need a lot of space for this activity and you might choose to do it outside.)

The DISC Profile

Did you notice that each of our new friends has character traits that resemble one of the four personality types in the DISC profile? It's described in more detail on the next page. Since you took the DISC yourself, can you pick out which of the four friends is most like you?

Seven Steps to Purpose

Congratulations! You are beginning the first step in discovering how God wired you. It is the intellectual, or mental phase of the process. You will begin to understand:
Your Personality Style
Your Resilience - or "Bounce Back"
Your Top 5 Core Values
Your Spiritual Gifts
Your Strongest Passions

Remember, in all of these assessments there are no right or wrong answers. Your goal is to get to know yourself better. With each assessment, you are adding another piece to your own purpose mosaic. Get ready to have some fun and learn more about the amazing person God created you to be!

You do the steps - And God does the rest!

⇨Object Lesson: How are You Wired?
You will need chenille wires and beads for each student.

We've learned a little more about how God created us in the last couple of weeks. To demonstrate that, each of you have *wires* and beads to work with to create your *"self-portrait."* Usually we make a portrait with a camera, or paint and a canvas, but today we want to create an object that says something about you. Be creative, have fun, and let your imagination speak through wires and beads.
Ask a few volunteers to share their artwork and describe the object they created and what it says about them.

Meet our Friends

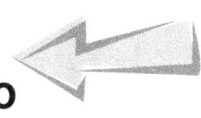

LEON
ACTION HERO

These friends are out-going, and full of energy. They can be emotional and they make quick decisions. They are likely to "take a dare."

REESE
COMEDIAN

Likes: To be in charge
Fears: Being taken advantage of
Under stress: Impatient
Strengths: Responsible, Lots of energy, Gets things done.
Dislikes: Rules, Impatient, Doesn't like to listen. Can start a fight.

Likes: Fun, and lots of friends.
Fears: Being disliked.
Under Stress: Disorganized.
Strengths: Friendly, funny, a good talker.
Dislikes: Has a hard time following instructions. Not a good listener. Cleaning their room.

Theses friends are all about getting the job done and doing it well.

Theses friends are the kind that want to be best friends. They love to help others.

Likes: To be perfect, Information.
Fears: Being criticized by others.
Under stress: Critical and picky.
Strengths: Open-minded, wants the facts, follows directions.
Dislikes: Negative attitude, stuck in details, doesn't like risks, misses the big picture.

Likes: Security, helping others and teamwork.
Fears: Loss of stability or security.
Under stress: Won't share.
Strengths: Understands others, warm and loyal, Follows directions, team player.
Dislikes: Change, multi-tasking, slow to respond to problems.

BRODIE
PRIVATE EYE

These friends are quiet and sometimes shy. They don't easily get excited about things and they are slow and steady when getting things done. They don't like change and they can be fearful.

GRACE
FAITHFUL SIDEKICK

WHICH CHARACTER IS MOST LIKE YOU?

Highlight the the description that best describes you. Use another color to highlight the area that describes you second best.

D = Dominant and Driver } The Action Hero
I = Influencing and Inspiring} The Comedian
S = Steady and Stable } The Faithful Sidekick
C = Correct and Compliant } The Private Eye

Do you have a favorite character? Is that character like you, or perhaps the opposite of you? There is a saying that opposites attract each other. That's likely because they are the best helpers to one another.

IDENTITY AND DESTINY
AMAZING KIDS FOR

Lesson 4

NAME: _____ DATE: _____

MEMORY VERSE: *Romans 12:4-5 Just as our bodies have many parts and each part has a special function, so it is with Christ's body. We are many parts of one body, and we all belong to each other.*

Write the verse here. Memorize it at home.

_____

_____

_____

MY BIG AHA!
1 Thessalonians 1:4 (TM) It is clear to us, friends, that God not only loves you very much but also has put his hand on you for something special.

When you think about this Scripture, recognize that your personality is part of the mosaic that God created you to be. He made you for something special, do you have an idea of what that ASSIGNMENT might be?

MOSAIC PIECE
ASSIGNMENT: It's what God is asking you to do next.

CAPTURE IT!
Which of the four new friends that we met today is most like you?

Leon is the D personality. He's outgoing and take's charge. He's bold when it comes to taking risks and he doesn't mind telling you what he thinks about things.

Reese is the I personality. She's cheerful, fun-loving, creative and talkative member of the group.

Grace is the S personality. She's soft-spoken, warm, caring and dependable. You can always count on her to do her part. She can be a little shy at times, but she's good at understanding and listening to others.

Brodie is the C personality. He's focused, precise, detailed and neat. He's a great problem solver, he's more task oriented than he is focused on people.

Which character is most like you?

_____

IDENTITY AND DESTINY
AMAZING KIDS FOR

Lesson 5

Memory Verse: **Ps. 139:14 Thank you for making me so wonderfully complex! Your workmanship is marvelous—how well I know it.**

Objective: To Find Out How You are Wired

⇨ **River Crossing**

After some discussion, the group of new friends decided to head toward the nearby trees. There was nothing close at hand that was suitable to help them get across the river, so the friends decided to explore the woods. They chatted and laughed as they walked along. As they approached the trees, Bernie ran ahead with his nose to the ground. He was suddenly aware of the scent of forest animals and wanted to find them. The woods grew very thick with a lot of bushes and undergrowth that quickly made it difficult to go very far. The friends noticed that the woods reached all the way down to the river in some places and they made their way to the first spot where the water reached up into the trees. "I'll bet this is why the river looks like iced tea," Brodie observed. "What do you mean?" Chris asked. These trees are cedar, can you smell how fragrant they are?" Brodie continued, "The cedar wood stains the water, some people call it cedar water." Zoé nodded, "We have cedar trees on my Dad's farm. It smells so good to add a few chips to your closet, or burn cedar in the fireplace in the winter."

Reese laughed, "Wow Brodie, you don't miss a thing do you?" She closed her eyes and smiled as she inhaled the pleasant smell; like incense, it reminded her of camping out and roasting marshmallows around an open fire. "Hey everybody," Leon called out, "I think we have a solution to our problem!" The friends all turned their attention to Leon. They rushed to help him and found that there were two canoes tucked in to the brush. They each had oars in them too. "Wow!" The kids were excited about the solution to their problem. The canoes were dirty and old but looked sound enough. Everyone helped to pull out the boats, brush dirt from them, settle who would ride in each of them, who could row,

MOSAIC PIECE

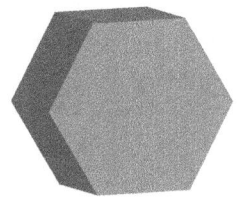

RESILIENCE:
"Bounce back."

and who could steer. Some of the friends couldn't swim, some had never been in a canoe, but others had experience with both, so once all was settled, the kids began to climb into the canoes. Chris and Leon were the last to jump in to each canoe and they pushed away from the bank and into the water, side by side.

Everyone shared the excitement of the next challenge in their adventure being solved. Bernie sat in the bottom of the canoe in front of Chris and happily barked as if he was talking to the group. As always, Perry was overhead, soaring, swooping, and occassionally landing on Zoé's arm. As the friends pulled away from the bank, Grace noticed that her feet were getting wet. She patted Bernie and continued talking and laughing with the others, thinking, "The bank of the river was muddy and wet and I must have gotten wet getting into the canoe." Before long, Bernie began to lick at Chris's feet, and Grace noticed that there seemed to be more water in the bottom of the canoe! She now realized that there was a slow leak in the bottom of the boat and she warned, "It looks like we're taking on water!" Leon called back, "How bad is it?" Grace replied, "I'm not sure!" She examined the bottom of the canoe more carefully and saw the water slowly seeping in through a seam in the wood. "I don't know how to swim!" She suddenly felt very frightened and wondered if they were going to make it across the river, the opposite bank still seemed very far away, and the water in the canoe was steadily getting deeper.

Lesson 5 page 2

⇨ **You are Fearfully and Wonderfully Made**

Ps. 139:14 Thank you for making me so wonderfully complex! Your workmanship is marvelous—how well I know it.

What do you do when you're afraid? Everyone feels afraid sometimes, but we don't all respond in the same way. Grace began to feel afraid when the water began to seep into the boat. She couldn't swim, it took her awhile to realize there was a problem, and what she wanted most was the security of the river bank. She froze because she didn't know what to do. Do you think Brodie, the problem solver, or Leon the action guy, would respond the same way Grace did?

Keep in mind that God made you unique and special. You have a basic personality that is not going to change much as you get older. It's what Coach Tom would call "factory installed."

You can learn your personality type at a young age and work with your strengths to move directly toward your purpose.

⇨ **Object Talk: RESILIENCE**
You will need an uncooked egg and a tennis ball.

Hold up the egg and the tennis ball for the class to see. "Which of these do you think is designed to hit the floor and bounce back? What will happen if I drop this egg on the floor? Do you remember the story of Humpty Dumpty? Do you think if this egg has a great fall we'll be able to put it back together again ? Would it be a good idea to use the egg on a tennis court; whack it across the net at my opponent? What is different about this tennis ball that makes it suitable for playing tennis? IT'S VERY BOUNCY! You can hit it all day it just bounces back. You can play in the heat, in the rain, in the gym, almost anywhere. If you try to bounce it in a pool it'll float to the top. It doesn't sink and it doesn't SPLAT! The tennis ball is a perfect example of resilience - or BOUNCE BACK.

⇨**Active Learning: River Crossing**

(There are several versions of this game available online.
Search for "River Crossing," to find both active games and video versions. This is a great game for strengthening problem solving skills, t eam building, leadership and communication skills.)

Form groups with each group consisting of five to ten members. The object of the game is that each team must cross a marked-out area using some type of stepping stones. The stones can be carpet tiles, or any object that the students can jump on, from one to the next.
Use 1 stepping stone for every third player. This will require the students to think through their crossing as a team. The stepping stones are to be used to cross the marked-out area, from start to finish. You can call your marked out area a river, to coordinate with today's story. A person must always be in contact with the stepping stone. The team must cross the area bringing all the stepping stones and team members along. The team crossing the area in the fastest time wins. (Try playing the game once without obstacles. Once the groups catch on to the concept, you can add additional obstacles and let them play again.)

Think about this:
God wants all of us to be on His team and play our part. When we find our purpose, we become the best players we can be.
When you have purpose you have energy, c onfidence, focus and fun!

God wants your life to be successful!

IDENTITY AND DESTINY

AMAZING KIDS FOR

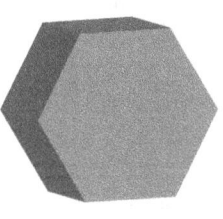

Lesson 5

NAME: _____ DATE: _____

MEMORY VERSE: Ps. 139:14 Thank you for making me so wonderfully complex! Your workmanship is marvelous; how well I know it.

Objective: Discover How you are Wired.
Write the verse here. Memorize it at home.

_____

_____

_____

MY BIG AHA!

Your basic personality won't change that much as you get older. As Coach Tom says, "It's factory installed." It's fun to learn about how God designed you and your friends. You'll see that all of you are slightly different in some ways. It's important to remember to show respect for others' unique person- ality style. **Do you remember your personality style from Lesson 3?**

How can you use your behavior style to help meet the needs of others?

MOSAIC PIECE

RESILIENCE: Being able to bounce back when you go through tough times.

CAPTURE IT!

Opposites Attract. Have you ever thought about your friends and family and realized that the people you are closest to often are very different from you? Do you think it's God's way of playing a funny trick on us? It's really more like God's perfect plan for us; to bring people into our lives to complement us in the areas that we are not as strong.

God created us to have relationships with others for our protection, for our growth, and for the opportunity to use our gifts and strengths to bless others.

Our friends can help us bounce back when we go through tough times. Think about your friends and family. Do you have someone special who helps you bounce back?

Do they have the same personality as you?

Are they opposite from you?

How do you help each other grow?

IDENTITY AND DESTINY
AMAZING KIDS *FOR*

Lesson 6

Memory Verse: **Ps. 139:14 Thank you for making me so wonderfully complex! Your workmanship is marvelous—how well I know it.**

Objective: To Find Out How You are Wired

⇨ **River Crossing - Part 2**

MOSAIC PIECE

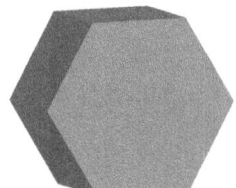

RESILIENCE:
"Bounce back."

Chris called out to the others, "We are going to turn around, this canoe won't make it across the river." Grace seemed a bit panicky so he assured her, "We can make it back to the bank and then some of the others can come back for us." Leon agreed that his boat would continue to cross and he and Reese would return for them. The adventurers were concerned about leaving anyone alone, but Zoé assured them, "With Perry by my side, I won't be alone. We will start building a fire while you finish the crossing," She looked at the sky as she said this and realized that it was late afternoon by now. Soon it would be dark and everyone was getting tired. She was thinking ahead and didn't say anymore, she didn't want to worry anyone with thoughts of the night in the woods.

Chris and Brodie safely made their way back to their starting point and helped Grace climb from the canoe. Brodie set out to see if he could find sap from trees, large leaves, or anything that he could use to repair the canoe. Bernie ran along beside him, happy to be back on dry ground, he had a mission of his own; he could smell the forest animals and he sniffed the ground and wagged his tail as he followed Brodie. Chris and Grace dumped the water from the canoe and studied the damage. It did seem to be a small leak and Chris thought that Brodie's idea might work if they could find the right materials to use. Grace pulled an energy bar and her canteen from her back pack and offered some to Chris, she then settled on the bank to survey the river and relax a little while. It was going to be a long wait.

Meanwhile, Leon and Reese were returning from the other side of the river. Zoé and Perry began to look

for firewood and a possible campsite. By the time Leon and Reese reached the riverbank, the shadows were getting longer. They were very tired from crossing the river twice, so it was decided that they would rest this time and Chris and Grace would row, while Reese sat in the middle. Brodie had not found enough tree sap to patch the other canoe, but he wasn't giving up, he continued to search and try other ideas. Leon helped him while the others made their way across the river. The crossing took about 30 minutes, which seemed much longer as the friends grew tired and the day was nearly spent. As soon as the canoe touched the bank, Zoé greeted them and welcomed Reese. Chris and Grace began the return trip to get the others and again took about 30 minutes to cross the river. They found Leon and Brodie still working on trying to fix the canoe. Grace was very tired by this time, so it was her turn to ride in the center of the boat while Leon and Brodie took the oars. Chris and Bernie waited on the bank and watched as the sun slowly sank toward the horizon. Chris pulled some jerky and water from his pack and he and Bernie had a snack while they waited. Bernie was a great companion and a watch dog too, so Chris was not worried about being alone. Chris could hear the splash of oars before he could see the returning canoe. Before long, Brodie and Leon returned. Chris hopped into the canoe and Bernie followed. At last, the three boys made their final trip across the water. All of the travelers were tired by now, and very thankful to be reunited as the moon began to shine on the river.

⇨ **Resilience - How well do you bounce back?**

Ps. 139:14 Thank you for making me so wonderfully complex! Your workmanship is marvelous—how well I know it.

In our story, the travelers needed to rely on their strengths to get them through the challenges of crossing the river, having little food and water, and being very tired from the strain of the day.

We are all stressed sometimes. That's when we find out of what we're really made. Resilience is the ability to bounce back when life is demanding. How strong are you emotionally? Can you change your bounce back? You sure can!

We're going to answer some questions that will help you see where you are emotionally strong, and where you can use some improvement.

Turn to the Bounce Back Questionnaire on the next page and allow the class to do their assessments. (*Note to the teacher - read the questions out loud along with the students to help them understand the questions when necessary.)

River Cross: Free - Logic Puzzle Game
By Steil
You will need access to the internet, a projector and a laptop.

Allow the class to take turns playing this game on the big screen. Alternate groups of students taking their assessments with students playing the game.

Try repeating the following river crossing game. Divide teams differently than the last game. Ask questions when the game is over: Did you notice any improvements in your game this time? Does it help to understand the way to succeed at the game, and how each player contributes to the team? This time put some obstacles in the way like chairs or other items that the students must go around , over, or under. Did the obstacles make the game harder? Did the students naturally gravitate to their strengths as D's, I's, S's, and C's? Discuss this at the end of the game.

⇨ **Active Learning: River Crossing**

You might like to repeat the river crossing game from Lesson 5, this time add obstacles to make it more challenging.

Think about this:
God wants all of us to be on His team and play our part. When we find our purpose, we become the best players we can be.

When you have purpose you have energy, confidence, focus and fun!

God wants your life to be successful!
You do the steps - God does the rest!

Bring some protein bars and jerky for the class to sample. Also bring a canteen or an individual "camel back" such as hikers use to carry water on their back. Show the kids how it works.
If you go hiking or on a wilderness adventure, be sure to be prepared. What items would you carry with you on a hike or a camp out? Why would you want those items? Allow several students the opportunity to respond.

Lesson 6 page 3

⇨ **RESILIENCE QUESTIONAIRE**

Your ability to "Bounce Back" is affected by seven different factors that we will look at one by one.

1. Emotional Self - Control: How well do you stay calm under pressure?
2. Impulse Control: How well do you control sudden, strong desires?
3. Optimism: A positive point of view.
4. Causal Recognition: The ability to identify the cause of your problems.
5. Empathy: Do you recognize someone else's feelings?
6. "I make a difference": The understanding that you have an effect on the world.
7. Reaching Out: Are you able to take risks and get to know people?

Read the following statements and choose the answer that is most like you. Circle or highlight your answer.

1. You are playing with building blocks with a friend and you have a very high, strong building almost completed. Suddenly your friend takes a big chunk out of your tower and says, "I need more blocks!"

A. You get very angry and punch your friend as you take the blocks back from him.

B. You are angry but you stop and count to 5. You think about what just happened and you say, "That's not very nice, you didn't have to take my blocks, we can get more from the closet."

2. You come home from school one day and smell something delicious as you enter the door. You walk into the kitchen and greet your mom who is just putting the frosting on a big chocolate cake. You try to stick your finger in the frosting but Mom says, "Not until after dinner!"

A. You wait until Mom leaves the kitchen and you stick your finger into the back of the cake hoping she won't notice. Yum! It's delicious!

B. You stare at the cake for a minute thinking about how good it will taste, it even makes your mouth water, but you turn to the refrigerator and get an apple instead.

3. You're sitting at your desk when the teacher announces, "Clear your desks, we're taking a Pop Quiz."

A. Your palms get sweaty and you worry, "I wish I had studied last night, I will probably fail this test!"

B. You take a deep breath as you clear your desk and say a silent prayer, "God I am not sure about this quiz but with your help I believe I can pass it."

4. Your soccer team has made it to the playoffs, you're in the final minutes of the game and your team is losing by one point. You are in position as the ball comes to you, taking aim you give the ball your best shot and, POW! The goalie deflects the ball and the horn sounds, ending the game.

A. You fall on the ground and start sobbing. You tell yourself, "We lost and it's all my fault. The team would be better off without me!"

B. Your shoulders slump and you feel disappointed. As one of your teammates approaches, you say, "Wow that was so close! I think if we practice hard we will beat them next year!"

5. You're at a friend's birthday party and everyone is laughing, playing games and having a great time. You notice a girl from your class sitting by herself and she's quieter than usual.

A. You don't pay much attention to her because you're involved in your game.

B. You notice the girl and you go over to talk to her. You ask, "Hi, are you okay? You seem very quiet today."

6. Think back to when you first learned how to ride a bike, or skate board, or another challenge that was very hard for you. Everytime you got on the bike you fell!

A. You got frustrated and gave up saying, "I'll never get this, it's too hard!"

B. You kept getting back up and trying again. You thought, "If I just keep trying, I'm going to ride this bike!"

7. Your Dad is being transferred to a new job in another city. You're sad because you have a lot of friends in your town and you will miss them a lot.

A. You doubt that you'll ever be able to get used to your new home and you just know you won't have any friends there. When you do meet some new kids, you stare at the floor and refuse to look at them because you still miss your old friends so much.

B. When you get to your new school, you're nervous and excited too. You smile as your teacher greets you and introduces you to your new classmates. She directs you to your seat and you smile at the classmate beside you as she whispers, "Hi! My name is Sarah, I'll be happy to show you around."

⇨ **How is your Bounce Back?**
Think about this: "bounce back" is one of the most important keys to success in life. It's your "thinking" style, your belief system; or the glasses through which you view the world.

On each of the seven areas that we looked at, there is a Scripture verse that goes with it. If you selected the A answer, or if you feel your answer is somewhere in the middle of the two examples, memorize and practice living the verse that goes with the example. Your "bounce back" can be strengthened with time and practice because you can change the way you think about things.

FOCUS:
God's promises + His presence = Bounce Back

"Don't copy the behavior and customs of this world, but let God transform you into a new person by changing the way you think." Romans 12.2

For each of the questions below, transfer the letter from your quiz to the line below. If you scored a B, you have good coping skills in that area. If you scored an A, or if you feel your answer should be somewhere in the middle, write M. Use the Scripture verses and write them down, memorize them and pray asking God to help you change the way you think.
1. Do I control my emotions? _____
2. Do I control sudden, strong desires? _____
3. How positive is my point of view? _____
4. Do I recognize the cause of my problems? _____
5. Do I identify with someone else's feelings? _____
6. Do I recognize that I make a difference? _____
7. Do I reach out to others? _____

1. **Philippians 4:6 "Don't be anxious about anything."**
People with good bounce back have the ability to stay calm under pressure and control their emotions.

2. **Matthew 26:41 "Pray so you do not fall into temptation."**
People with good impulse control are able to stop before they act. They can wait for the things they want, and they can say "No" to temptation.

3. **1 Thessalonians 5:16 "Be joyful always, pray continually, give thanks in all circumstances."**
Optimistic people see their future as being bright. God wants us to have a positive outlook on life.

4. **Psalm 139:23 "Search me, oh God, and know my heart."**
People with good bounce back can identify the cause of their problems without falling into extremes like depression or anxiety.

5. **Zechariah 7:9 "Show mercy and compassion to one another."**
Empathy is your ability to feel for others and show that you care about what they care about.

6. **Hebrews 12:1 "Run with perseverance the race set before you."**
People who know they make a difference make very good leaders. They believe they can solve problems, and they have faith that they can succeed in what they do.

7. **Psalm 34:4 "I looked for the Lord and He answered me. He saved me from all my fears."**
Reaching out is a skill that requires you to get past your fear of people and your fear of failure. Fear is a paralyzing emotion and it can keep you from doing what God asks you to do. He's always ready to help you.

IDENTITY AND DESTINY

AMAZING KIDS  FOR

Lesson 6

NAME: _____ DATE: _____

MEMORY VERSE: *"Don't copy the behavior and customs of this world, but let God transform you into a new person by changing the way you think."* Romans 12.2

Objective: Discover How you are Wired.

God's promises + His presence = Bounce Back!

Use the small box to write the area of bounce back that you want to change. Write the memory verse on the lines. Ask God to help you change the way you think. Practice the verse every day!

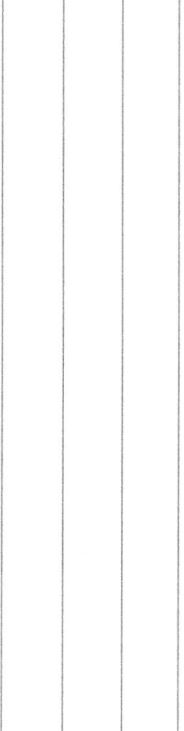

MOSAIC PIECE

RESILIENCE: Being able to bounce back when you go through tough times.

MY BIG AHA! Results from your Bounce Back Questions

Write your answer to each of the seven areas in your quiz, either A, B, or M meaning somewhere in the middle, on the line by each example.

1. Emotional Self - Control: How well do you stay calm under pressure?
Philippians 4:6 "Don't be anxious about anything." _____
People with good bounce back have the ability to stay calm under pressure and control their emotions.

2. Impulse Control: How well do you control sudden, strong desires?
Matthew 26:41 "Pray so you do not fall into temptation." _____
People with good impulse control are able to stop before they act. They can wait for the things they want, and they can say "No" to temptation.

3. Optimism: A positive point of view.
1 Thessalonians 5:16 "Be joyful always, pray continually, give thanks in all circumstances." _____
Optimistic people see their future as being bright. God wants us to have a positive outlook on life.

4. Causal Recognition: The ability to recognize the cause of your problems.
Psalm 139:23 "Search me, oh God, and know my heart." _____
People with good bounce back can identify the cause of their problems without falling into extremes like depression or anxiety.

5. Empathy: Do you recognize someone else's feelings?
Zechariah 7:9 "Show mercy and compassion to one another." _____
Empathy is your ability to feel for others and show that you care about what they care about.

6. "I make a difference": I have an effect on the world.
Hebrews 12:1 "Run with perseverance the race set before you." _____
People who know they make a difference make very good leaders. They believe they can solve problems, and they have faith that they can succeed in what they do.

7. Reaching Out: Are you able to take risks and get to know people?
Psalm 34:4 "I looked for the Lord and He answered me. He saved me from all my fears." _____
Reaching out is a skill that requires you to get past your fear of people and your fear of failure. Fear is a paralyzing emotion and it can keep you from doing what God asks you to do. He's always ready to help you.

IDENTITY AND DESTINY
AMAZING KIDS *FOR*

Lesson 7

Memory Verse: 1 Corinthians: 13
And now these three remain: faith, hope and love. But the greatest of these is love.

Objective: To Find Out How You are Wired

⇨ **A Night in the Woods**

Chris climbed out of the canoe and although he was extremely tired, he also felt a rush of excitement as he realized that the new friends had together tackled another challenge in their journey. His sense of adventure kept him focused on making it through to the end; wherever that might be. So far, this journey had been one unknown challenge after another and none of them had been alike. Now the six friends were reunited on the opposite bank and they were in a mood for celebration. They felt like a team that just won a championship game.

Zoé had a nice fire blazing on the bank which helped each of the travelers find one another as they crossed over the river. Grace smiled, more relaxed now that all the friends were together again. Reese and Leon told their stories about the crossing, and everyone congratulated Brodie on his diligence at trying to patch the leaky canoe. As the friends shared stories, and snacks from their backpacks, they rested around the roaring campfire. After awhile they became quiet as the long day and physical exertion began to take affect. Zoé began to sing a folk song, soft and lilting, the sound was beautiful and mysterious. One by one the friends joined in, caught up in the beauty of the evening and the warmth of the campfire. As the last note trailed off, they heard a loud snore. Brodie had fallen asleep as if his friends had been singing a lullaby. Bernie stirred, and barked softly, he had been asleep too. The friends burst into laughter and Brodie sat upright, startled, "What! What's happened?" The travelers laughed again, and Brodie rubbed his eyes and straightened his glasses.

MOSAIC PIECE

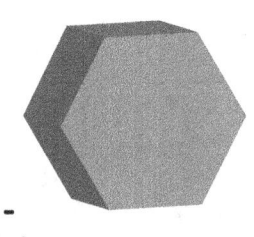

VALUES:
Belief that is special or the most important - What you want the most.

At last, Chris wondered aloud what they had all been secretly thinking, "What next?" No one answered for awhile. It seemed safe and cozy by the fire. Should the party risk wandering in woods at night? Perhaps getting split up and lost, not knowing where they were and having no clue which way to go next. The thought of sleeping in the woods was frightening to Reese. She had never camped out before and this whole adventure seemed to challenge her in ways that she had never experienced. The thought of wandering in the woods at night was even more spooky. At least here by the bank of the river they had a bright fire, the soft glow of moonlight, and the company of friends. She felt much safer staying right by the fire. Brodie felt so tired that he wanted to rest before they moved on. Leon felt that they would be better off moving ahead and trying to figure out where they were. Grace was just happy to be safe and warm. Her experience on the river crossing had been enough for her for one day. She was willing to go along with the majority decision but she hoped they would stay put until daylight.

Zoé spoke to Perry her falcon, "Go check things out girl." Perry had been dozing on Zoé's shoulder but she obediently stretched her wings, fluffed her feathers, and lifted off over the tree tops.

The friends sat silently for a few minutes, thinking about their options. They could hear the sounds of a night owl and some rustling in the leaves that was probably a raccoon, opossum, or other foraging creature. The sounds made Reese a little nervous, and she moved a little closer to the fire.

Lesson 7 page 2

Each of the six travelers in our story had a different idea about what to do next and why.

Which idea did you prefer? Or would you have another solution to, "What's next?" That's another example of how we often think differently than our friends or family members because we all have different priorities - or, what matters the most to us.

⇨ CORE VALUES KEEP YOU ON COURSE

Core Values are your deeply held beliefs. They are what matters most to you. Can you imagine riding on a train with no track? Can you imagine riding on a go-cart track with no guard rails? What would that be like? Living without core values would be like that. A curvy, mountain road without guard rails is a formula for disaster.

You need strong beliefs, they are like a compass, so that when peer pressure, tough choices, or other people's expectations come up; you'll make good decisions. People without strong core values are described in the book of James like this:

**"A wave of the sea, blown and tossed by the wind... double-minded and unstable."
James 1:7-8**

Our memory verse today is a good example of some important core values. "Faith, hope and love, and the greatest of these is love." 1 Cor. 13:13.

If you have trouble figuring out your core values, the Bible is the best source for finding out what God's core values are. When we steer according to God's values, we have a track to ride on, or a road with guardrails.

Demonstrate this by using a clear baking dish with water in it nearly to the top of the pan. Use a large lego block or a toy boat and float it on the water. Next use a fan to blow across the face of the water. The air stirs the water and causes the boat to toss and turn losing its direction.

How is this boat doing when there is no wind blowing? It does okay doesn't it? But what happens when the wind starts to blow? Having strong core values will keep you on course when troubles come because they work like a rudder, used to steer the boat to stay on course.

⇨ Active Learning: Filters and Prisms

Use the internet to find science experiments and crafts that demonstrate how filters and prisms work. **Use several glasses of different sizes and pour water into them at different levels. Experiment, shining a flashlight on the glasses to watch as a prism effect is created. Darken the room for effect.**

As we think about how filters and prisms work, we realize that they affect the light that passes through them. Pure white light is separated into a rainbow of color when passed through a prism. Is the light still white? Yes it is, but it is broken into its various components based on the length of the waves that form each color in the spectrum.

The Bible says that God is light. Think about His love shining to us as pure white light. We are like the prisms and filters that His light passes through. Each of us has different core values, strengths and gifts. As God's light passes through us, we reflect His nature in a rainbow of different ways. This is one way to describe how we need each other in the Body of Christ. When we bring our strengths and talents and values together, we reflect a more true and accurate picture of the pure white light that is God's glory.

Use coffee filters and water soluble markers to create designs. Allow the students to create their own designs. Open the filters up flat and color only the pleated parts of the filter. Leave the center circle plain. Fold the filter into 1/4's and dip the tip of the filter in a glass of water. Watch as the water absorbs into the filter causing the colors to run and spread. Open the filters and lay them flat on paper towels to dry.

Notice how unique and beautiful each project is. They are all different - just like we are all different.

IDENTITY AND DESTINY
AMAZING KIDS FOR

Lesson 7

NAME: _____   DATE: _____

MEMORY VERSE: 1 Corinthians 13:13 "And now these three remain: faith, hope and love. But the greatest of these is love."

Write the verse here.
Memorize it at home.

Objective: Begin to Discover Your Purpose Mosaic

MOSAIC PIECE

VALUES: Belief that is special or the most important what you want the most.

CAPTURE IT! Core values can be compared to a prism or a filter. They affect the way you view life. God wants us to see others as He sees them: with the filter of love, and the prism of faith and hope.

MY BIG AHA! Core Values are your deeply held beliefs. They are what matters most to you. Can you imagine riding on a train with no track? What would that be like? Living without core values would be like that. You need strong beliefs, they are like a compass, so that when peer pressure, tough choices, or other people's expectations come up; you'll make good decisions. People without strong core values are described in the book of James like this: **"A wave of the sea, blown and tossed by the wind; double-minded and unstable."** James 1:7-8

What are some of your core values?

IDENTITY AND DESTINY
AMAZING KIDS FOR

Lesson 8

Memory Verse: **1 Corinthians 13:13**
And now these three remain: faith, hope and love. But the greatest of these is love.

Objective: To Find Out What Makes You Tick

⇨ **A Night in the Woods part 2**

After some discussion it was agreed that the best thing to do in the unfamiliar woods was to stay by the campfire. The campers decided to take turns sleeping while two at a time kept watch and kept the fire going. Leon and Reese were too wound up to rest so they agreed to take the first watch while the rest of the group settled down to relax using their packs as pillows. Some had jackets some did not but the fire provided plenty of warmth. Leon stayed close by, but gathered more dry sticks and branches to keep the fire hot.

The woods sang with the hum of crickets and cicadas, owls and whippoorwills, and rustling in the leaves and branches. It was like a lullaby and the weary campers dropped off to sleep one by one. Grace was still fearful. This day and its events had taken a toll. She whispered to Zoé, "Are you asleep?" "Hmm, almost," Zoé whispered back, "Are you okay?" Grace nodded in the dark and sighed, "I'm trying to be. I've never been so tired and afraid in my whole life." Zoé understood. Grace didn't grow up with nature in her backyard, campouts in the woods, and several brothers to teach her survival skills. "It's okay," she assured her new friend. "We are safe next to the fire, and we can't be too far from a town or something. Everything will look brighter after we've rested for the night." Grace tried to smile and she admired how brave Zoé was. "I'm not really so brave, Grace, I just have a lot of experience at camping out. We'll be fine, you'll see. Now try to sleep." Grace nodded, "Thanks Zoé, I'll try."

As she said this a wolf howled in the distance. That was a new sound. Grace shot straight up, "What's that?"

MOSAIC PIECE

VALUES:
Belief that is special or the most important - What you want the most.

"It's a wolf," Zoé replied. Leon and Reese were a little nervous too. They were from the suburbs and only heard wolves howl on scary movies. Chris and Brodie stirred too. "As long as we keep our fire going we'll be fine. It keeps us warm but also keeps prowling animals away." Chris yawned and turned over with his back to the fire. "Leon, why don't you rest for awhile, and I'll watch." Grace thought that was a good idea. She offered to let Reese sleep, "I'm wide awake now, I might as well take a turn." Chris stretched as he stood up and picked up some more sticks for the fire.

A couple of hours passed and everyone slept. Chris dozed, his head bobbing down on his chest. Bernie began to growl. He woke Chris with a low, "Ruff, ruff!" and another growl. His ears were perked up and his fur stood up on his neck. "What is it boy?" Chris was awake now. The fire had died down low and Chris quickly added more wood and stirred the embers to help it catch. As the fire blazed up again he could see a raccoon, foraging around getting closer to the packs that the travelers carried. Bernie barked and the coon waddled away. "That fat coon sure looks well fed." Chris patted Bernie, "Thanks boy, you did your job."

Zoé and Brodie took the last watch of the night with no more incidents. The sun began to rise and color the sky pink and pale orange. Birds began to twitter in the trees and the woods felt more friendly. The campers yawned and stretched and wondered what this new day would bring.

HOW DO WE DEVELOP CORE VALUES?

Core Values are your deeply held beliefs. They are what matters most to you.
Where do you think we learn about the things that matter most to us?
Some of our core values are learned from our parents. They pass some of their values on to us. Some of our core values are developed by our teachers, and by the things we experience in life.
Someone who has been hurt by a friend might develop a strong need for loyalty. This would be considered a "SHOULD" core value because it is developed by the pressures of the world around you. The expectations of other people, and our own pride or ego can cause us to adopt some "SHOULD" values too. A SHOULD CORE VALUE is developed to protect yourself, please others, or make a way to feel good about yourself.

A "CHOSEN" CORE VALUE is one that you consciously choose because it really matters alot.
In order to determine what our CHOSEN CORE VALUES are, we must think and listen with our heart.

ESTABLISHING CORE VALUES

Go through the the words provided on the word sheets, each with a brief definition. Make copies of the pages and cut the word blocks out and provide a set for each student. Optional: you may choose to let the students work in pairs. Allow the students to compare word #1 with word #2 and select the one that matters most to them. Continue with #3 and #4 and so on.
Next ask the students to eliminate the next tier of cards by comparing the choice from selection 1 or 2, with the selection from choice 3 or 4. Continue this process and eliminate cards until the student has only 5 cards left.

⇨ **Active Learning:**

Provide markers, crayons, colored pencils, and coffee filters for each student.
Use a paper circle, or coffee filters and fold into 5 sections. Write each of the core values that you chose on one of the sections. Color the sections different colors. Draw a picture or write a name or an object in the section that reminds you of that core value.

Use the journal page to write the top 5 core values, each one on a differnt point of the star printed on the page. Allow the students to color the points, or draw on them.

Remind the class that Jesus should be at the center of our core values. This represents that we have asked Him to be our Lord and Savior and we want His values to be ours too.

CAPTURE IT!
Core values can be compared to a prism or a filter. They affect the way you view life.
Using the Bible as a source for finding your core values will help you fulfill God's purpose for your life and view life through God's filter, or point of view.

Lesson 8 page 3

WORD LIST

1. ACCEPTANCE
Approval from others

2. ACCOUNTABILITY
Responsible.

3. ACHIEVEMENT
Doing great things.

4. ATTITUDE
Point of view.

5. AUTHENTIC
Real.

6. BALANCE
Stable and sure.

7. BOLDNESS
Confident and fearless.

8. CHARACTER
Quality personality.

9. COMMITMENT
You can count on me!

10. COMPASSION
Care about others.

11. COMPETENCE
Good at what you do.

12. CONTENTMENT
Satisfied.

13. COURAGE
Do what's right even when you're afraid.

14. CREATIVITY
Enjoy beautiful things.

15. DEVOTION
Love and faithfulness.

16. DISCIPLINE
Self-control and training.

17. DISCOVERY
Adventure, learning new things.

18. DIVERSITY
Many different parts.

19. EMPATHY
Identify with the feelings of others.

WORD LIST

20. ENDURANCE
Able to continue even in suffering.

21. ENTHUSIASM
Eager and intense.

22. EXCELLENCE
Exceptional quality.

23. FAIRNESS
Everyone treated equally.

24. FAMILY
Relatives.

25. FITNESS
Healthy and in good shape.

26. GENEROSITY
Willing to share what you have.

27. GENTLENESS
Tender and kind. Calm and friendly.

28. GROWTH
Making progress.

29. HONESTY
Truthful.

30. HONOR
Respect.

31. HOPE
Expectant trust.

32. HUMILITY
Strength under control. Put others first.

33. HUMOR
See the funny side of things.

34. INDEPENDENCE
Freedom, liberty.

35. INTIMACY
Close friendship, someone you can trust with your secrets.

36. JOY
Happiness that comes from deep inside.

37. JUSTICE
Fairness.

38. KINDNESS
Good and merciful.

Lesson 8 page 5

WORD LIST

39. LEADERSHIP
Able to take charge and direct others.

40. LEARNING
Eager to know more.

41. LOVE
Unconditional devotion.

42. LOYALTY
Constant and dependable.

43. OBEDIENCE
LIsten and do what you're told.

44. ORDER
Everything in its proper place.

45. PATIENCE
Willing to wait.

46. PEACE
Calm.

47. PERSEVERANCE
Never quit.

48. QUALITY
Only the best.

49. RELATIONSHIPS
Friends and family.

50. RESPECT
Treat others with honor.

51. SACRIFICE
Willing to give until it hurts.

52. SECURITY
Safe and sound.

53. SIMPLICITY
Pure and easy.

54. SPIRITUALITY
Close friends with God.

55. TEAMWORK
Many hands = light work.

56. THANKFULNESS
Grateful for what you have.

57. TRUTH
Real, right and exact.

58. WISDOM
Deep knowledge that comes from God.

IDENTITY AND DESTINY

AMAZING KIDS FOR

Lesson 8

NAME: _____ DATE: _____

MEMORY VERSE: 1 Corinthians 13:13 "And now these three remain: faith, hope and love. But the greatest of these is love."

Write the verse here.
Memorize it at home.

Objective: Begin to Discover Your Purpose Mosaic

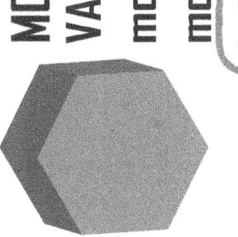

MOSAIC PIECE

VALUES: Belief that is special or the most important or what you want the most.

CAPTURE IT! Core values can be compared to a prism or a filter. They affect the way you view life. Using the Bible as a source for finding your core values will help you fulfill God's purpose for your life and view life through God's filter, or point of view.

MY BIG AHA! Core Values are your deeply held beliefs. They are what matters most to you. You need strong beliefs. They are like a compass, so that when peer pressure, tough choices, or other people's expectations come up; you'll make good decisions.

After today's exercise, you should be able to define your top 5 core values. Write them in the segments of the star.

Jesus should be at the center of your core values. Put His name in the center of your star.

IDENTITY AND DESTINY
AMAZING KIDS FOR

Lesson 9

Memory Verse: **1 Peter 4:10 Each one should use whatever gift he has received to serve others, faithfully administering God's grace in its various forms.**

Objective: To Find Out What Makes you Tick

⇨ **What a Difference a Day Makes**

Leon rummaged through his pack. He had one energy bar and half of his canteen of water. The campers knew that they had to make their food and water stretch because they had no idea when they would find more. Everyone was ready to start out and hike again so Chris stirred the ashes of the fire with a stick to make sure that all of the embers were out. "What's this?" He wondered as he saw a glimmer in the coals. He used his stick and uncovered a shiny, black piece of rock. "Wow! Looks like I have another piece for my collection." He carefully lifted the rock making sure it wasn't hot. Brushing it off he admired the light reflecting from the rock, "It's even prettier when it's not all dirty." The others joined him and admired the piece. One by one they began to find their own pieces of black rock to remember this event.

Reese began to hum and then sing as the group started to hike deeper into the woods. Soon, they all joined in and felt the excitement as they considered that they had just accomplished another phase of their adventure. Their song was interrupted when Perry swooped down and perched on Zoé's arm. "What's ahead girl? Did you see anything?" Perry cawed and flew up into the sky again. She was heading deeper into the woods and the group agreed to follow her. Perry led the group to a berry patch in a clearing where the hungry travelers were able to fill their hands with ripe berries. Reese was amazed that it was possible to find food in the woods. Zoé laughed and shook her head in wonder. "How do city folks survive?" she wondered silently.

MOSAIC PIECE

SPIRITUAL GIFTS: Special abilities given to us by God to equip us to serve others.

The hikers were encouraged by the knowledge that Perry was an excellent guide. They began to relax and sing once again. They shared stories about their adventures and joked and laughed together about some of the things they experienced. Time passed and the sun rose in the sky. The hikers still trudged on and some were starting to get tired. Everyone agreed to take a break and they dropped their packs and rested against some trees in the shade. The day was starting to get warm and the need for water was becoming a concern. Most of the boys and girls still had a little bit in their canteens but they were afraid to drink much of it until they could find a source of fresh water. As they rested, it became very quiet as one by one the travelers closed their eyes and reflected on their own personal thoughts. Chris dozed off for a few minutes when he heard a stir among his companions. "What was that?" Brodie asked. An unusual sound carried across the air and everyone listened now. The sound of a horn lingered in the air. "I wonder what that was?" "Where is it coming from?" The boys and girls were wide awake now and ready to find the source of the noise they had heard. It seemed they must be close to civilization, but what was it? "I wonder if that was a call to lunch at a camp," Chris thought aloud. "Or a military base, " Leon offered. "Or a prison camp!" Brodie worried. "Now stop that, Brodie," Reese scolded as she saw the look of panic cross Grace's face. "I'm sure it's nothing as dreadful as that. " Everyone agreed to head in the direction of the noise to find out its source.

As the group of kids continue their journey they each respond to situations differently. Some are more cautious, some more adventurous. Some are very resourceful and some like teamwork.

We learned about personality types and how this affects our responses in situations. Next we will look at **SPIRITUAL GIFTS.**

These are special strengths and abilities given to believers by God. We all have spiritual gifts that equip us to fulfill our purpose.

As we grow up we learn to correct our mistakes and focus on areas that we need to improve. Our parents, teachers, and coaches point out the things we do wrong so that we can correct them.

In this class we want to focus on what we do well.

When you focus and build upon your strengths, you are focused on positive things.

1. You focus on your blessings.

2. You appreciate the "YOU" that God wants you to be.

3. You guard your heart and mind from wanting to be like others.

4. You allow yourself to put your gifts to their best use.

It's all about being the amazing YOU God created!

Let's look at your spiritual gifts and learn more about what makes you tick.

⇨**Active Learning:**

DISCOVERING YOUR SPIRITUAL GIFTS

Bill Gothard, founder of the Institute of Basic Life Principles said, "As we exercise our gifts, we experience personal fulfillment and a deep sense of joy. By concentrating on our gifts, we achieve maximum fruitfulness with minimum weariness."

We do our best when we do the things we are good at doing. The Spiritual Gifts Quiz on the next page is modified from several sources, worded for kids and will help them discover what their spiritual gifts are.
People tend to have more than one spiritual gift. The ones with the highest scores are called your **SPIRITUAL GIFT SET.**
For more information on Spiritual Gifts tests, see the internet for several free resources.

For younger children it is helpful for an adult to read the statements and help the student score the quiz.

Think about this...

Have you ever dreamed about what you would like to be when you grow up? Your spiritual gifts are a good way to learn what careers you could be very good at. When you do a job that God designed you to do well, it's easy to love what you do. At the end of the quiz, you will find a description for seven different spiritual gifts and the kinds of jobs that people with this gift tend to do very well.

Think about whether you have ever desired to do some of the things described in your spiritual gift set. When you think about what you would like to be when you grow up, take some time to research that career. What kind of school will your dream job require? Will you need to go to college? What can you do now to prepare for your dream?

SPIRITUAL GIFTS QUIZ

Answer the following questions with a number from 0 - 3. Be as honest as you can.
     0=not at all, 1=a little bit, 2=some, 3=a lot.

1. I like to say things that help other people feel better and stronger. _____

2. I like to help people with the things they need. _____

3. I like to tell people about Jesus, about the Bible, and how it applies to their life. _____

4. I like to apply Bible truths to situations in my own life. _____

5. Other kids tell me that I have helped them understand the Bible better. _____

6. When people are sad, I like to say things that help them feel better. _____

7. I am not afraid to tell others about Jesus. _____

8. I am good at saving my money. I like to share with others and give to the church. _____

9. I like helping my parents, teachers, and pastors get jobs done so they can do the things they need to do. _____

10. I like helping kids who have handicaps and special needs. _____

11. I have no problem finding ways to get odd jobs to earn money. _____

12. I like to encourage people when they feel afraid. _____

13. I can encourage others to get involved in order to get a job done. _____

14. When there is a job to be done, I am happy to help. _____

15. My friends usually make me the group leader when we do things together as a team. _____

16. I'm good at organizing things; like my room and my closet. I like things neat. _____

17. I like to pray for people when they need healing. _____

18. I love to give to missions or help with special projects to serve others. _____

19. When someone is sad or crying, it makes me feel sad too. _____

20. Sometimes when I pray, I get a feeling about what God wants to say to me. _____

21. I enjoy helping around the house, at school, and at my church. _____

Transfer your scores to the following page beside the number that matches it in order to learn what your spiritual gifts are. You will have 3 numbers for each category. Add the numbers together to see which are the highest totals.

Lesson 9 page 4

SPIRITUAL GIFTS RESULTS

The next step in your spiritual gifts quiz is to write the numbers that you assigned to each statement in the line beside the number of the question. In other words, if you scored a 2 on question 1, write 2 on the line beside question 1. Complete this step for each question.

1. _____   8. _____   15. _____

2. _____   9. _____   16. _____

3. _____   10. _____   17. _____

4. _____   11. _____   18. _____

5. _____   12. _____   19. _____

6. _____   13. _____   20. _____

7. _____   14. _____   21. _____

The next step in your discovery process is to add the results in the following groups of numbers together. (Example: 1. (2) + 7. (1) + 20. (2) = (5)

The score for this group of numbers is (5).

Group 1.   1._____ + 7._____ + 20._____ = _____

Group 2.   2._____ + 14._____ + 21._____ = _____

Group 3.   3._____ + 4._____ + 5._____ = _____

Group 4.   6._____ + 12._____ + 13._____ = _____

Group 5.   8._____ + 11._____ + 18._____ = _____

Group 6.   9._____ + 15._____ + 16._____ = _____

Group 7.   10._____ + 17._____ + 19._____ = _____

Group 1. *Prophet* A person with this gift is good at talking to people and sharing valuable information with them. They have insight into spiritual things.
Banking, investing, business, government and world issues are some of the things that a person with this spiritual gift can be very good at doing.

Group 2. *Server* People who are self-motivated and gifted at tasks that require skill with their hands. People with this special gift are happy when they can help others accomplish projects.
Builders, athletes, chefs, photograpers and artists are some examples of people who are talented in this area.

Group 3. *Teacher* People who enjoy searching for truth and sharing it with others have this spiritual gift.
Research scientists dig deep for truth, archaeologists, and professors often have this special ability from God.

Group 4. *Exhorter* Some people have a special way of being able to cheer others up when they are down.
Counselors need this gift from God, and so do leaders. Even people who work as comedians, circus clowns, and actors are motivated by this special skill.

Group 5. *Giver* The special ability to earn money in order to give generously.
Some business people and investors have this talent.

Group 6. *Organizer* People with the ability to see the details of a project and help all of the aspects of the planning work together to complete the goals. Most businesses and organizations need people who can manage and take care of all the details in order to meet deadlines and achieve goals.

Group 7. *Mercy* Some people have a special way of helping others who are hurting. They may work in nursing homes, and with handicapped, special needs, very sick people, or people who have experienced disaster. Doctors, nurses, pastors, missionaries, Red Cross volunteers, and many others have this gift.

IDENTITY AND DESTINY
AMAZING KIDS FOR

Lesson 9

NAME: _____ DATE: _____

MEMORY VERSE: 1 Peter 4:10 "Each one should use whatever gift he has received to serve others, faithfully administering God's grace in its various forms."

Write the verse here.

Memorize it at home.

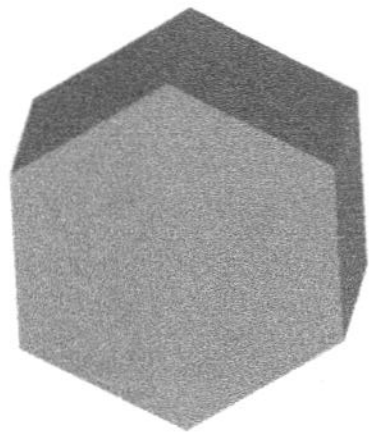

MOSAIC PIECE

SPIRITUAL GIFTS: Special abilities given to us by God to equip us to serve others.

CAPTURE IT! Spiritual gifts come directly from God and are an important part of how you have been uniquely created to accomplish your God-given purpose.

MY BIG AHA!   SPIRITUAL GIFTS DISCOVERY

Complete the quiz on pages 3 and 4. Write in the totals that you scored for each group. On which group did you score the highest? Put a star beside it on the list below:

Group 1: **PROPHET** _____   Group 2: **SERVER** _____
Group 3: **TEACHER** _____   Group 4: **EXHORTER** _____
Group 5: **GIVER** _____   Group 6: **ORGANIZER** _____
Group 7: **MERCY** _____

Everyone has a main gift and some 2nd and 3rd gifts. What were your second highest and third highest scores? Circle the 2nd highest score and the 3rd highest score.

What are some ways that you use your spiritual gifts? Use the hexagon space to describe your gifts and how you use them.

IDENTITY AND DESTINY
AMAZING KIDS FOR

Lesson 10

Memory Verse: **Romans 11:29**
"For God's gifts and His call can never be withdrawn."

Objective: To Find Out What's Your Passion

⇨ **Welcome to Camp**

The hikers began to move toward the sound of the horn they heard. Perry flew ahead and returned to Zoé's shoulder. Back and forth, Perry flew and led the group to a clearing where several cabins were arranged around an open field. The boys and girls were certain now that they had discovered civilization. They were excited to find people after such a long day but they were nervous too. What if the people weren't friendly? They were almost out of food and water and had no other choice but to press on and take their chances.

The compound area was empty, in fact the camp looked deserted and except for the horn they had heard, Brodie worried they weren't going to find people here at all. Leon spotted the main office cabin and he figured it would be the place to start in order to find some answers. As the group climbed the stairs and opened the door they were amazed to see Coach Tom talking to another coach dressed in the same uniform. The two turned and saw the group and they were delighted. "Wow, you have no idea how worried we've been!" Coach Tom explained that he was preparing to send out a search party for this group of hikers that had been missing for almost 24 hours. The travelers exchanged confused looks as they all thought that their adventure was part of the challenge they were to complete. Chris was the first to speak, "Wow Coach, you have no idea how glad we are that we have come upon friends."
All of the kids agreed. It seemed their journey had made all of them cautious but ready to tackle whatever came up next.

MOSAIC PIECE
PASSION:
A strong, driving feeling, conviction or desire.

Coach Tom introduced Coach Pam, "She's a member of our team here at Camp I & D." The kids looked puzzled and Leon asked, "I & D?" Coach Tom chuckled, "Identity and Destiny. Sorry, we use a lot of acronyms." Everyone exchanged greetings and Leon nodded his understanding.
"We're so glad you're here," Coach Pam shook everyone's hand warmly and shared a welcoming smile. The group began to relax as she explained that they had not intended for these hikers to be gone so long. "All of the other campers were led back here with their clues after the soccer game. I have been so worried about all of you." Coach Tom added, "Well, are all of you okay? Is anyone hurt?" The travelers assured him that they were fine. "The next order of business is to get you all to the chow hall, you must be starving!" The kids laughed and agreed that they could use a good meal. "That's it then, let's get you a meal, and get you settled, then we'll bring you up to date on the activities and the counselors here." Coach Tom was all business and he was determined to get the hikers settled in as quickly as possible. Coach Pam smiled and added, "Come on everybody follow me, I'll show you where the dining hall is located." Bernie barked then and Coach Pam laughed, "You too boy, I'm sure we can find something you'll like."

PASSION PURSUIT

Passion is very strong emotion, like love or hate. In this lesson we will take step 3 of our journey and learn about how passion and purpose are linked together.

What are you passionate about? This is a good clue to what your purpose may be. Think about:

❶ Past events and accomplishments.
❷ Things that you want to accomplish in your life.
❸ People who have influenced you.
❹ Wrongs that you would like to make right.

We'll also look at the underlying needs and desires that your passions address, the common themes that run through them, and the ways they point to your God-given purpose.

JOURNAL PAGE

Allow the students to answer the passion pursuit questions on their journal page.

Give examples of things that kids might be passionate about to help fuel their creativity. Ideas: Sports awards, honor roll, perfect attendance. What they want to be when they grow up. Favorite teachers, athletes, relatives, actors, singers. Causes such as; say no to drugs, gangs and bullies, Jump Rope for Heart, and others. Favorite hobbies, games and past times. What are some things they absolutely hate? Ideas such as bullying, or exclusive cliques at school. Some may feel passionate about poverty or childhood illness. Kids are exposed to many things via T.V. and internet. Share an example of something from your own life that you are passionate about. Identify the need beneath the passion and explain that to the class.

Ask the class if they can understand why they feel so strongly about some of their choices. Perhaps they have personal experience in their own family, or at school, or perhaps their church or school sponsors certain organizations in which the students have been involved.

⇨**Active Learning:**

WHO AM I?

Provide a headband for each student. (These can be made from strips of fabric and tied around the forehead.)
Make several career and identity cards on 3x5 cards before class so that each student has a different identity on their card. Don't let the students see their card, but place it in their head band so that others can read it.
To play the game the students must ask questions of their fellow players in order to guess the career, or identity on their card. They can only ask questions that require a "Yes" or "No" answer. The first student to correctly identify their card is the winner. If time permits you can shuffle the cards and give the students an opportunity to play again. Try playing the game in small groups of 4 - 5, and try playing it with the entire group for variety.

When the game is over ask the students to consider the cards they were given. Do you think you would ever want to be the career person that was on your card? Why, or why not? What career do you want to pursue?

Another option is to create a set of cards with causes, situations, and events that stir passion in a child's heart. Allow the class to play the game with each set of cards, or even mix the cards together and let the class guess if their card is a passion or a career.
Use the list of examples provided on this page to generate ideas.

Career Suggestions:

Doctor	Lawyer	Teacher
Pastor	Parent	Policeman
Fireman	Dancer	Sales Person
Actor	Singer	Baseball Player
Scientist	Astronaut	Airplane Pilot
Soldier	Baker	Business Owner
Chef	Gymnast	Fitness Coach

Passion Suggestions:
Missions Locally, Leading people to Jesus, Missions in Foreign Countries, Causes such as Jump Rope for Heart, or Relay for Life, Say "No" to Drugs, Helping the elderly (Boy Scouts and Girl Scouts)
Health and Physical Fitness, Family Relationships, Sports.

IDENTITY AND DESTINY
AMAZING KIDS  FOR

Lesson 10

NAME: _____ DATE: _____

MEMORY VERSE: Jeremiah 1:5 TMB "Before I shaped you in the womb, I knew all about you. Before you saw the light of day, I had holy plans for you." *Write the verse here. Memorize it at home.*
Objective: Passion Pursuit

MOSAIC PIECE
PASSION: A strong, driving feeling, conviction or desire.

CAPTURE IT!
There is a link between passion and purpose. God has a plan for your life. The things that you feel very strongly about are clues to understanding your purpose.

MY BIG AHA! Passion can be a strong like, or strong dislike for something. Use the heart on this page to write about something that you LOVE! Not like ice cream or pizza, but think about this question when you write: What would you do to create meaning in your life if time and money were unlimited?

Use the space in this box to write about something that makes you really angry.

IDENTITY AND DESTINY
AMAZING KIDS *FOR*

Lesson 11

Memory Verse: **Romans 11:29**
"For God's gifts and His call can never be withdrawn."

Objective: To Find Out What's Your Passion

⇨ **Welcome to Camp part 2**

Chris was a little surprised that Coach Pam seemed to know him. He had never met her before and didn't remember Camp I & D at all. He looked at Zoé and shrugged. Happy to be in a safe place with the promise of a good meal, he wasn't too concerned about whether he remembered the place. The travelers all followed Coach Pam to the dining hall. Several other campers were already there noisily enjoying their lunches. Coach Pam led the way to the kitchen where the trays were ready to be filled with good food and cartons of milk. They found a table with enough seats for them to sit together. The band of wanderers had developed a special friendship during their adventure and they wanted to stick together. They felt somehow safer and more secure that way. The friends were so hungry they were about to dive into their lunches when Coach Pam cleared her throat, "Ahem! Can we bless the food first please?" Leon looked apologetic, "Yes ma'am," he replied and all of the friends bowed their heads. "Coach Pam prayed, "Lord, thank You for watching over these boys and girls and bringing them to us safely. Bless their time here at Camp I&D and bless this food now in Jesus' name, amen." "Amen!" The friends replied together and they quickly turned to their lunch trays as if they hadn't eaten in weeks. Some of the other campers began to gather around them, full of questions and concerns. It seemed the wanderers had become something of a legend. Everyone wanted to know how they got lost and then how they found their way to the camp. Zoé recognized some of the campers as members of her Dodge Ball team. Was that just yesterday? So much happened in the last 24 hours that it seemed like days had passed.

MOSAIC PIECE

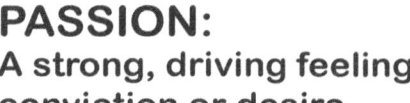

PASSION:
A strong, driving feeling, conviction or desire.

Chris enjoyed all of the attention and so did Reese and Leon. Brody and Grace on the other hand felt shy and embarrassed. Brody studied his lunch tray and didn't say much, while Grace sat a little closer to Zoé for security. Chris shared tales of his adventure. He told about the clues and following Perry to find direction. He talked about how his boat had a leak and he had to return to the shore instead of crossing the river. He made sure that everyone knew that he was not afraid even when he and Bernie were alone in the woods. Some of the campers were not so sure about his brave words. Leon and Reese admitted that the whole thing was scary at times but they felt safe when they stayed together.

Coach Tom came to the dining hall then and he blew his whistle, "TWEET! Okay everybody, time for afternoon activities, let's head to the gym." The campers all followed Coach Tom as he led the way. As they stepped out into the sun, Chris saw Bernie, happily napping in the shade of a big oak tree. Bernie had a full belly and a contented smile as he slept. They heard a familiar, "Caw, caw," as Perry swooped down and rested on Zoé's arm. "Good girl," Zoé stroked Perry's neck and smiled. With her help, the campers found their way through the clues and the woods all the way to the camp ground. "Do you think we would have made it here without her help?" Zoé asked Chris. "I don't know," Chris shook his head, "I'm just glad we didn't have to." Zoé agreed, "Me too." Then their new friends chimed in, "Me too!" They all laughed as they headed toward the gym and whatever Coach Tom had for them next.

PASSION OR PURPOSE?

Passion is very strong emotion, like love or hate. It can help give us clues to our purpose but it is not the same thing as purpose. Imagine if you were only led by your passions. Emotion can be tricky and misleading so we have to be careful to be sure that our passion is properly directed.

What is purpose? Something set up as an object or result to be achieved. We set goals to achieve our purpose.
If you want to be a professional athlete, what kinds of goals must you set to achieve the purpose? How does passion help you fulfill your goals?
What if you want to be a doctor, or a lawyer? What goals must you complete? It takes a lot of hard work to accomplish our purpose. Without passion we can lose our focus and our momentum and give up when things get difficult. Passion helps to "fuel your engine" to keep you going. Without purpose, passion can lead you in the wrong direction. So it takes both working together to accomplish our God-given destiny.

⇨ Active Learning:

The Apostle Paul is a great example of a man with passion and purpose. We read alot about him in the book of Acts. First known as Saul of Tarsus, he was a fierce defender of the Jewish faith and he strictly obeyed the law to the point that he made a mistake. He was PASSIONATE about God's Law. When people began to follow Jesus, he believed they were breaking the law. In his zeal, he put Christians in jail and even killed some of them.
Do you think his passion was leading him in the right direction? read Acts 9:1 "Saul was uttering threats with every breath and was eager to kill the Lord's followers." One day as he was on the road traveling to Damascus on a mission to hunt down Christians, a bright light shone from heaven. Saul was knocked off of his horse and blinded by the light. He heard Jesus say to him, "Why are you persecuting me?" Saul answered, "Who are you?" And the voice replied, "I am Jesus."

Saul was a changed man after that. He took his orders from Jesus and used his passion to fulfill his God-given purpose. He preached everywhere he went and he wrote most of the books in the New Testament. As much as he had persecuted others, there were many other fervent Jews who persecuted him. He suffered beatings, prison time, ship wrecks, and he was even left for dead. Paul's passion kept him going. He never stopped preaching the good news about Jesus. From his prison cell he wrote to the growing churches to be joyful, keep the faith, and keep doing what's right.

Bean Bag Toss with a Twist

Use several been bags or balls for tossing and a basket. Place the basket at one end of the play area and use masking tape to make a starting line about 10 feet from the basket. Divide the class into two teams. The first team is on the side of the room with the basket. The second team is at the starting line with the bean bags or balls. The first player on team 2 tosses a bean bag and tries to get it in the basket. The player from team 1 tries to hit the bag away from the basket to prevent it from getting in. Allow each player on each team to take a turn.

Count the number of bags that made it into the basket. Next reverse roles and allow team 1 to try to get the bags into the basket and team 2 tries to bat the bags away. Add up the total of bags this time. The team with the highest number of bags in the basket wins.

Ask the class some questions after the game. How did it feel trying to get the bags into the basket when the opponent was knocking the bags away? Did you feel like giving up? Did you get angry?
When we try to achieve our goals and accomplish our purpose, we can often feel like we are being challenged with every step. If that's the case, we have to allow our passion for our purpose to keep us encouraged and motivated to do what's right.
When you know you're on the right track, it doesn't mean it will be easy. Keep at it, and don't quit. God will help you accomplish your goals just like He helped Apostle Paul spread the Gospel all over the world. (Gospel means "Good News".) Why is the truth about Jesus good news? Who can you share the gospel with today and tomorrow? That will be part of our purpose as Christians.

IDENTITY AND DESTINY

AMAZING KIDS FOR

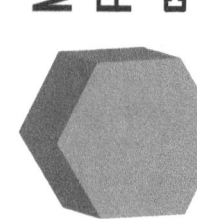

Lesson 11

NAME: _____ DATE: _____

MEMORY VERSE: Romans 11:29 "For God's gifts and His call can never be withdrawn."

Write the verse here. Memorize it at home.

Objective: Passion Pursuit

List at least 3 things that you know you are very good at doing.

1.

2.

3.

What do you want to be when you grow up? List 3 things.

1.

2.

3.

Name 3 people that you look up to.

1.

2.

3.

MOSAIC PIECE

PASSION: A strong, driving feeling, conviction or desire.

CAPTURE IT!

Let's look at some questions that will help you identify the powerful feelings that you have. As you dig deeper into these emotions, the Lord will help you to discover your passions.

Take a Deeper Look

What need does your passion fulfill in you? Ask yourself why the things you listed are important to you. Do you like rewards when you do a good job? Do you want to make a difference in life, or need to feel accepted by others? The "WHY QUESTIONS" help show what's in our heart. If you've ever heard someone say their heart is on fire for Jesus, you now know what they are describing - PASSION.

IDENTITY AND DESTINY
AMAZING KIDS *FOR*

Lesson 12

Memory Verse: **Psalm 139:16**
"All the days ordained for me were written in Your book before one of them came to be."

Objective: To Find Out What's Stopping You

⇨ **The Bridge**

As the campers entered the gym, they all found seats in the bleachers. Coach Tom was there, ready to start the afternoon activities. He was all business as he said, "Okay everybody lets get started." Chris and Zoé were intrigued to be part of a camp and wanted to learn what was next. Zoé sat on the edge of her seat and leaned forward to catch every word as Coach Tom began.

"We talked alot about passion in our last session and today we are going to take one more look at it before we move on to the next topic. Think about your parent's car for a minute. Have you ever noticed the lights on the dashboard? What do those lights indicate?" A tall boy called out, "When the red light comes on it means if you don't get to the gas station soon for a fill-up your car is going to stop!" The campers all laughed. Coach Tom asked, "So you've had some experience with that huh?" The boy replied, "Yes sir! And that was not fun." Other campers replied, "There's an oil light," "A blue light that says your bright lights are on," "The speedometer shows how fast you're going."
Coach Tom nodded, "All those are very good answers. Now think of your passions that you've learned about and think of them as the lights on your dashboard. When your passion light goes on, it's indicating what's going on under the hood. The brighter the light, the stronger the passion and the more likely that there is a strong need in you that this passion fulfills.
Let's look at a few questions before we hit the next activity.

MOSAIC PIECE

NEED: Something necessary or required, useful, or desirable.

Several camp leaders began passing out papers to all of the campers. Everyone was given a pencil and Coach Tom instructed, "This page of your journal is all about what excites you, makes you happy, makes you feel good, or gives you satisfaction.

(Turn to journal page 12 and allow the class to do the exercise.)

As the campers completed the page, Coach Tom said, "We've spent the last several days learning about 5 major things:
1 Your Primary Personality Style
2 How Resilient You Are
3 Your Top 5 Core Values
4 Your Dominant Spiritual Gift
5 Your Passion and the Needs that Live Beneath the Passion
Together these concepts paint a picture of the amazing person that God designed you to be. You've learned a lot about yourself! That's very important if you want to be successful in life."

Chris realized that the journey that he and Zoé had taken had taught him a lot about himself, his personality, his strengths, his fears, and his ability to work together as a team member under pressure. He was amazed that he was right on track with the lesson that Coach Tom was presenting. He looked at Zoé and his four new friends and grinned at them. "We've been through a challenge that taught us a lot about what's under our hood." The friends all agreed, and exchanged hugs and "high five's."

At Camp I&D the next exercise takes place in the camp chapel. If you have a similar place available its perfect for this reflection time. If not, set up a quiet classroom with soft, meditation music and dimmed lights.

⇨**Active Learning:**

THERE'S PURPOSE IN THE PAIN
Remember our lesson about the Apostle Paul? He did a lot of wonderful things for God, but he also did some terrible things before he finally, "Saw the light." God uses the good things in our lives to build us up but He also uses the bad things to help teach us a better way. Think about Chris, Zoé, and their friends. It turned out that they were never supposed to get lost in the woods, but Chris realized that he learned a lot about himself in that struggle. That's what God can do with the struggles, pains, and difficult times that you have experienced. God promises to comfort you and provide for you. He'll take away the junk and rebuild your life, even in places that were destroyed for generations.
(Isaiah 61:3-4 paraphrased)
That's how much God loves us!

Sometimes people blame God when bad things happen. They ask, "If God is so loving, why did He let this happen to me?"
We must realize that we live in a sinful world. People do bad things and they hurt each other. That makes God very sad. Your own mistakes and poor choices can cause bad things to happen to you. But God loves you enough to forgive you and help turn your life around.

God is able to do even more than you can ever imagine like the Bible says in Ephesians 3:20-21.

Think about some things in your life that have caused you pain. Think about some things you've done wrong.
As we quietly listen to the music and think about these things, ask God to forgive you. Jesus died for your sins so that you can be forgiven.

Now think about this; for every negative in your life, God provides a solution.

As you think quietly fill in the blank in these next statements:
God is...............
God will ....
I need God to...........
Remember God has a plan for you that is unique. Only you can do it. Don't let the pains and mistakes you've made keep you from your God-given purpose.
It may seem that we've talked alot about you and how you are made. We know that God doesn't want us to be focused on ourselves all the time, but He's called us to serve others.
During this first part of finding your purpose, we have discovered how you can best serve others, by serving from your strengths.

Crossing the Bridge Game

Remember the story of the Three Billy Goats Gruff? (Remind the class of the folk tale; available online.)
In our story we must cross the bridge but the trolls under the bridge are called the 3 Amigos. Yes, they are friends, but they are not always YOUR friends. Their names are, Picky, Whatever, and That's Wrong! These 3 Amigos like to play under the bridge that you must cross to get to greener grass, bigger opportunities, and the purpose that God has for you.
What happens if you try to step onto the bridge and an Amigo pops up? You have to have an answer for his grumpy attitude, his attempt to distract you, or his ability to talk you out of your plan.
In our game last week you learned that as you try to accomplish a goal, (getting the ball into the basket,) there is often an obstacle to get past. The same applies to these 3 Amigos who rise in your own mind. Have you ever wanted to try something new and suddenly a voice pops in your head, "You can't do that, what are you thinking?" That's an Amigo voice. The thoughts that are critical, skeptical and judgmental will keep you from moving forward. We have to get past those thoughts to achieve our goals. (The same negative thoughts can also keep us out of trouble sometimes. How do we know the difference?) We'll learn about that when we cross the bridge.

Lesson 12 page 3

⇨ **REVIEW GAME**
(answer key is in the appendix)

The review game, Purpose in the Pain exercise, and the journal page exercise work well as alternating activities in a "centers" format. Divide the class into 3 groups and allow about 15 minutes for each activity.

Play a bridge crossing game by asking the students review questions. When they answer correctly they may take a step across the bridge. Since there are 3 trolls, or "amigos" you must answer 3 questions correctly to cross safely over the bridge.

Online problem solving games are also available. You might ask a review question and if the student answers correctly, they are permitted to take a turn at the video "Bridge Crossing Game."
You might prefer to set up a "bridge" by roping off an area in the classroom and allowing the students to take turns answering 3 questions. Those who answer all 3 questions correctly cross the bridge and earn a prize.

1. Emotional Regulation "How well you control your emotions" is a good thing to have.
TRUE OR FALSE?
2. In our story about Chris and Zoé, our friends begin an adventure by choosing to take a road that everyone travels.
TRUE OR FALSE?
3. God created you to be unique, or _____ of a kind.
4. Optimism means " A positive point of view."
TRUE OR FALSE?
5. In one of our memory verses, Jer. 29:11 we learned that God has a special _____ for our lives.
6. Destiny is what you _____ just by being you.
7. John 10:10 says God's _____ is to give us a rich and satisfying life.
8. In the river crossing, Chris and his friends learned how to work together as a _____.
9. An assignment is something that you buy at the store.
TRUE OR FALSE?
10. The Action Hero personality, like Leon, is a shy and fearful.
TRUE OR FALSE?
11. Resilience, or "bounce back" is the ability to "splat like an egg" when you hit the floor.
TRUE OR FALSE?

12. Core Values are beliefs that are special to you and that matter the most to you.
TRUE OR FALSE?
13. The Bible says that God is Light. When we allow His love to shine through us, we reflect his light to others.
TRUE OR FALSE?
14. 1 Cor. 13:13 ...The greatest of these is_____.
15. Core Values can be compared to a _____. They affect the way you view life.
16. Name one of your Core Values. _____
(Answers will vary. See Lesson 8 for examples.)
17. Spiritual gifts are special gifts given by God to every believer.
TRUE OR FALSE?
18. An example of a Spiritual Gift is a new bike for Christmas.
TRUE OR FALSE?
19. 1 Peter 4:10 Each one should use whatever gift he has received to _____ others.
20. _____ is a strong, driving feeling or desire.
21. Passion will help you focus on your goals and help you to achieve your purpose.
TRUE OR FALSE?
22. Romans 11:29 "For God's _____ and his call can never be withdrawn."
23. Coach Tom and Coach Pam allowed Chris and his friends to get lost on purpose so they would learn a lesson.
TRUE OR FALSE?
24. God doesn't want you to learn about how He designed you because He likes to keep things a MYSTERY.
TRUE OR FALSE?
25. In our lesson about the Apostle Paul we learned that there is no guarantee that you will not face obstacles when you are pursuing God's purpose for your life.
TRUE OR FALSE?
26. Discovering your passions, purpose, personality, spiritual gifts, and destiny are compared to gathering pieces of your own personal mosaic.
TRUE OR FALSE?
27. What is a mosaic?
Answers will vary.
Key words: beautiful artwork, stained glass window, unique, art made from several small glass shapes.

IDENTITY AND DESTINY

AMAZING KIDS FOR

Lesson 12

NAME: _____ DATE: _____

MEMORY VERSE: Psalm 139:16 "All the days ordained for me were written in Your book before one of them came to be."

Write the verse here.
Memorize it at home.

Objective: Passion Pursuit

MOSAIC PIECE
NEED: Something necessary or required, useful, or desirable.

CAPTURE IT! Discover the Greater Needs

Are there some common themes in your passions and the needs that inspire them? Look for words, patterns, and places where you see connections. Do some words cause a strong reaction when you think of them? Be sure to write them in the journal block below.

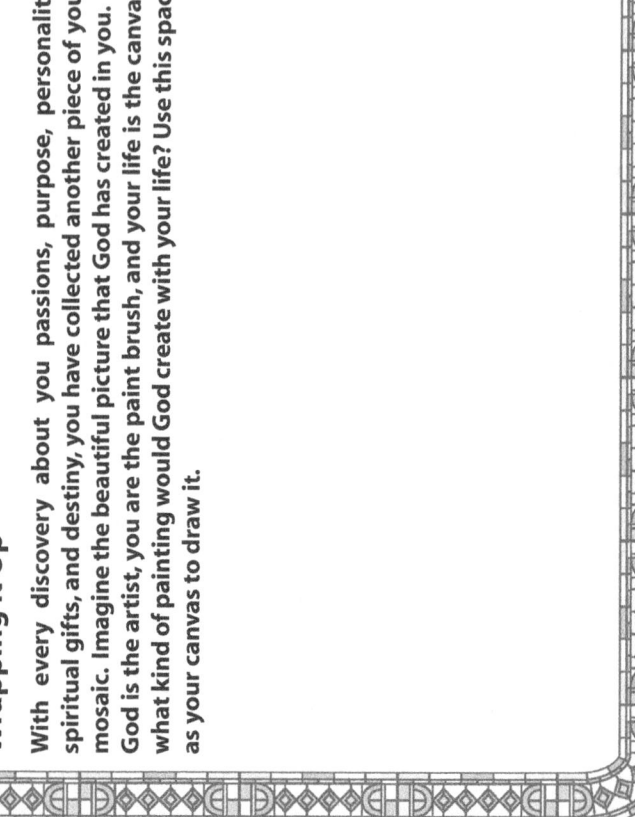

Wrapping it Up

With every discovery about you passions, purpose, personality, spiritual gifts, and destiny, you have collected another piece of your mosaic. Imagine the beautiful picture that God has created in you. If God is the artist, you are the paint brush, and your life is the canvas; what kind of painting would God create with your life? Use this space as your canvas to draw it.

Needs Beneath the Passion
Finish the following sentences:

I feel excited when I am doing _____

I like spending time with _____

I like helping _____

I like having _____ with my friends.

My favorite thing to do is: _____

My favorite place to go is _____

Create your own sentence: _____
_____

IDENTITY AND DESTINY
AMAZING KIDS *FOR*

Lesson 13

Memory Verse: **Isaiah 41:10**
"Do not fear, for I am with you, do not be dismayed, for I am your God. I will strengthen you and help you."

Objective: To Find Out What's Stopping You

⇨ **The Three Amigos**

Coach Tom blew his whistle. By now everyone realized that this meant something different was underway. He announced in his loud and clear voice, "We are now ready to face an obstacle course," The campers were excited, they loved the physical challenges at Camp I&D. Coach Tom blew his whistle again, "Alright everybody, listen up!" The gym was buzzing with conversation. "We're going to compete in an exercise that will require you to stay focused. You're going to be tested to see if you'll give up when the going gets tough. Let's all head outside."

⇨ **Active Learning: The Obstacle Course**

Create a course, either indoors with enough space, or outdoors. Create several obstacles to go through, over, around, or under using common items like card board boxes, chairs, rope, and any other items you might have. Enlist a few helpers to create diversions and obstacles along the course, like water guns, silly string, placing themselves on the path requiring the student to take a detour. Add some challenges to the course by requiring the students to complete a task at some of the obstacles; such as stacking cups, build a 25 piece puzzle, knock over some plastic bottles with a bean bag, or toss a bean bag through a hole. Make sure that the challenges are fun and engaging - use your imagination to add more obstacles if you like. Time the students to see who completes it the fastest.
OPTION:
Create 2 courses and divide class into 2 teams. See which team finishes first.

MOSAIC PIECE

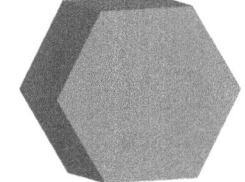

ROAD BLOCK:
An obstacle that keeps you from reaching your goal.

Discussion

Snacks and drinks will help the class settle down for this part of the lesson. Ask some questions:
How did you like the obstacle course? Was it fun or frustrating?
Did you feel like quitting sometimes?
Did you get angry when road blocks kept you from moving ahead?

This exercise was fun and at the same time we want you to learn from it. As you press on toward your goal of achieving your purpose, there will be obstacles, road blocks, detours, and even pitfalls.

Be ready when these things happen.

Little problems can be the hardest to overcome because they take your focus off of your goal. Sometimes life just seems busy, busy, busy, and we wonder if we'll ever get to achieve our goals. In fact we can become our own biggest road block when we allow ourselves to listen to the voices of the Three Amigos. These are the thoughts in our head that tell us what we can't do, and why we can't do it. Coach Tom calls them, "Critical, Skeptical, and Judgmental." You might know them better as, "Picky, Whatever, and That's just wrong!" These guys are Amigos when they keep us out of trouble, but they can also talk us out of doing the things we need to do to fulfill our calling from God. Let's look at our journal page to see what road blocks you're facing.
Turn to Journal Page 13

THE WHAT IF...... ROAD BLOCKS

Have you ever been too afraid to do what you needed to do?

For example, your teacher asks you to sit next to a new student and help them get familiar with the class routine. Do you think, "Sure, that's no problem!" Or do you think to yourself, "Why did the teacher pick me to do this? What if the new girl doesn't like me?" "What if she's mean and says things that hurt my feelings?" "What if the new girl thinks I don't know what I'm talking about?" Or, "I don't want to be bothered."

What if your Mom asks you to take cookies to the new neighbors, do a chore that you're not sure you can do well, or babysit a little brother for a few minutes while she makes dinner?

What examples can you name that cause you to get a case of the "What ifs?"

These thoughts are motivated by FEAR.
What does God say to us about fear? Over and over we are commanded, "Don't be afraid!"
God is with us to give us the power to do what is right.

We are all going to experience the nagging voice in our head that tries to stop us from fulfilling our purpose. Here are some "What ifs," that you might face.
What if I don't like my purpose once God reveals it to me?
What if I have to make BIG changes?
What if its too risky or dangerous?
What if it's not important enough for anyone to notice?
What if I can't do what it takes to complete my purpose?
What if I have to give up my friends, or my hobbies?
What if I'm wrong about my purpose?
What if I can't find my purpose?
What if people make fun of me?
What if I fail?

That's a lot of "What ifs," and most people are affected by some of them, not usually all of them. Which of the "What ifs," troubles you?

How about this one "What if I don't deserve to find my purpose?"

Have you ever wondered how or why God would ever want to use you?
That's called **UNWORTHINESS**

Stop and think for a minute about what the Bible says about it.
1 No one is worthy - only Jesus.
2 That's why He died for our sins.
3 We must accept His sacrifice and be forgiven for our sins.
4 God uses our mistakes and teaches us to help others as a result of it. He doesn't waste anything!
5 To think that Jesus can't love and forgive you because of what you have done is PRIDE.
Does it seem upside down to say that feeling like I'm not good enough is pride?
Remember - you are God's child and His love and sacrifice are enough for you.
To reject God's gift of salvation is like saying, "Jesus died for all sins but mine are too big for Him."

THINK ABOUT IT

Remember the Apostle Peter? He was a simple fisherman and he was good at "putting his foot in his mouth." He said things that showed he didn't really understand his purpose. He also made choices that got him into trouble. When Jesus was being questioned by the authorities, Peter even denied that he knew Jesus; not once, but three times! And yet Jesus still forgave Peter and chose him to help establish the church.

SPIRITUAL EXERCISE

Use a blank page in the appendix in the back of your book to write a prayer to Jesus. Do you need to ask Him for forgiveness, or maybe courage to obey and fulfill your purpose?
Write to Him about the "What ifs," that you face. Ask Him for His help so that you can do His will for you.

IDENTITY AND DESTINY
AMAZING KIDS FOR

Lesson 13

NAME: _____ DATE: _____

MEMORY VERSE: Isaiah 41:10 "Do not fear, for I am with you, do not be dismayed, for I am your God. I will strengthen you and help you."

Objective: What's Stopping You?

Write the verse here. _____

Memorize it at home.

MOSAIC PIECE

ROAD BLOCK: An obstacle that keeps you from reaching your goal.

CAPTURE IT! Look at it this way

Remember the Apostle Peter? He denied Christ 3 times when Jesus was captured by the soldiers, yet Jesus still chose him to have an important role in building the church. What would have happened if Peter rejected the purpose that God had for him?

Wrapping it Up

What was your biggest road block? Why is it your biggest concern?

_____

God wants you to be a success!

Read through the list of road blocks and rank them from 1, the one that is most important to you, to 7, the one that is least important to you.

____ **Satisfaction:** Life is good, I don't want to change it.

____ **Complacency:** Change is too hard. It's not worth it.

____ **Unbelief:** I'm not really sure God has a plan for my life.

____ **Fear:** What if I can't do what God wants me to do? I'm not sure I'm ready.

____ **Procrastination:** What's the hurry? Maybe when I'm older I'll try.

____ **Unwillingness:** I don't want to know what God's purpose is for me.

____ **Unworthiness:** How can God use me? I don't deserve it because of the things I've done wrong.

IDENTITY AND DESTINY
AMAZING KIDS FOR

Lesson 14

Memory Verse: Ephesians 6:10
"Be strong in the Lord and in His mighty power. Put on the full armor of God so that you can take a stand against the devil's schemes."

Objective: To Find Out What's Stopping You

⇨ **BATTLE FOR THE SOUL**

After the campers completed the obstacle course, Coach Tom invited them to all sit in the shade of a grove of trees. Bottles of water filled several coolers and the campers helped themselves to cold water as they sat in the shade. Chris and Zoé sat with their friends and laughed together about some of the challenges that they enjoyed during the exercise. Coach Pam joined the campers and she asked for everyone's attention. "We all learned some valuable lessons in our obstacle course today but I want you to think about something more. The obstacles were fun, and the course was like a game, but the truth is, the road blocks, fears and obstacles that get in our way to prevent us from achieving our purpose are all part of the Battle for our Soul. Real life obstacles aren't much fun and you need to be warned that they exist and you will have to overcome them. We want to take a little detour now to prepare you to be armed and ready for the obstacles that will come."

"We are moving into the spiritual part of our discovery process," Coach Tom added. "As we do, we will continue to ask the Lord to reveal your purpose, but you will find there are other things in addition to your fears and road blocks that get in the way."

Coach Pam nodded, "These obstacles are far more subtle and equally as important as the things we've already discussed." Coach Tom added, "As an example; you may find the daily, little problems become more difficult. Small things seem like big problems, and you may find that you are too busy to seek God for His will on a daily basis.

MOSAIC PIECE

ROAD BLOCK:
An obstacle that keeps you from reaching your goal.

We want you to be aware that there is an unseen spiritual power that tries to keep you from finding God's will."
Here's the plan as you seek God's will for you:
1. Know that there will be resistance spiritually.
2. PRAY! Ask God for wisdom, protection and strength.
3. Be prepared! Sometimes you may have to use some will power and keep putting one foot in front of the other to push through the obstacles.
4. Trust God! Know that he has wonderful things in store for you.
5. When you feel like giving up, get excited about your future. "Change the way you are thinking."
6. Remember: Your job is to stay on course and finish the race!

A DIFFERENT KIND OF BATTLE

What comes to your mind when you think of a battle? Do you imagine tanks, bomber planes and modern warfare? Do you picture knights on horses with long spears and armor? When we think of spiritual warfare we need to think about the battle for our mind; our thoughts and our feelings. This battle ground is in what the Bible calls our soul. We are made in 3 parts, in the image of God. God is our heavenly Father, Jesus is the Son, and the Holy Spirit is the 3rd part of God. We are created as a spiritual being, we have a mind and we live in a body.
Ever since Adam and Eve, there has been a spiritual battle and Satan is the enemy of our souls.
(See diagram on the journal page.)

YOUR AMAZING 3 PART BEING

As an object lesson, have a hard boiled egg and an apple on hand, as well as a knife to cut the apple.

Let's look at the journal page together and identify the 3 circles on the page. You are a spirit, you have a soul; your mind and emotions, and you live in a body. What happens when you die? Your body dies, but your soul and your spirit live forever. When you ask Jesus to be your savior, these are the parts of you that go to heaven. The Bible says that you will get a new body in heaven.

If it seems complicated to understand your 3 parts let's look at these 2 objects. The apple has 3 parts too. (Cut the apple as you share.) The outer skin is like your body, it's the part we see. The inside fruit is like our soul; our mind and emotions aren't immediately visible but they are easy to discover when we talk or behave in certain ways. The seed of the apple is like our spirit. It's deep inside and well hidden. Protected by our outer cover, it's also the part of us that bears fruit. When you plant the apple seed, a tree grows, eventually giving many more apples. When we ask Holy Spirit to give us His power, we are given gifts and talents to accomplish God's purpose for our lives.

What about the egg? It has a shell, an egg white, and a yolk, which is the seed of the egg. Crack open the egg to demonstrate. If we were to crack you open, we would be able to see your brain, it houses your mental functions, but we would not see your spirit. It's the invisible part of you, just like the Holy Spirit is invisible. We don't see the spirit, so how do we know He's real? Because we see the effects of the Spirit. We feel the strength of Holy Spirit fill us when we are afraid. We ask Him for help - and He gives it.

YOUR BATTLE PLAN

Let's look at how the spiritual battle is fought and won. The most common fight is the one in our head. Our mind says, "This makes no sense." While our spirit says, "Trust God and His promises."

How do we protect ourselves in a battle?
The Bible describes the armor that soldiers wear in a war. The battle that we fight is a spiritual battle that can be compared to physical warfare. Every part of the armor is designed to protect part of the body. What does the helmet protect? Our brain, our mind. So the helmet of salvation protects our soul. What about the breastplate of righteousness? It protects our heart and organs, or our feelings. The shield deflects the arrows of the devil and our sword is how we fight back; with the Word of God. Let's look at how that works.

FEAR
FALSE EVIDENCE APPEARING REAL

Using fear tactics is one of the devil's favorite tricks. Fear keeps you from doing God's will or obeying His voice. If God whispers in your ear, "Go talk to the new girl and help her feel welcome." What kinds of thoughts might go through your mind? Do you feel shy, or too busy, or you don't feel comfortable around strangers? Or maybe you ignore the nudge because God's voice is so subtle. Maybe you feel like you just can't be bothered.
Those thoughts are triggered by fears.
The Word of God is like a sword. It helps us combat all the wrong thoughts and ideas that pop into our head.
When we memorize Bible verses, they can pop up in our heads the minute the fear statements start.
"God will never leave you." "Fear not!" "Don't worry about anything, but pray with thanksgiving and God will give you peace."
Do you know that "Fear not!" appears at least 365 times in the Bible? That's once for every day of the year.
What are some of the fears that hold you back?

THE DARK ROOM
Use a clip from the internet to demonstrate how dark room photography development works.
Fear is like our own, personal dark room. When negative thoughts pop into our heads, and we take them to our dark room, they begin to develop, take form and become a clear picture.
What happens if someone opens the door to a photographer's dark room while the negatives are being developed? The pictures get ruined!
In the case of our negative thoughts and our dark room of fear, we want the light of truth to shine in and ruin the negative plans that could take shape.

IDENTITY AND DESTINY
AMAZING KIDS FOR

Lesson 14

NAME: _____ DATE: _____

MEMORY VERSE: Ephesians 6:10 "Be strong in the Lord and in His mighty power. Put on the full armor of God so that you can take a stand against the devil's schemes."

Write the verse here.

Memorize it at home.

Objective: What's Stopping You?

MOSAIC PIECE
ROAD BLOCK: An obstacle that keeps you from reaching your goal.

CAPTURE IT! One Person Three Parts

God is Father, Son, and Holy Spirit. We too have 3 distinct and connected parts to our being. We are a spiritual being, with a soul; which is our mind, will and emotions, and we live in a physical body. The body and the spirit want to control our mind which becomes our "battle ground."

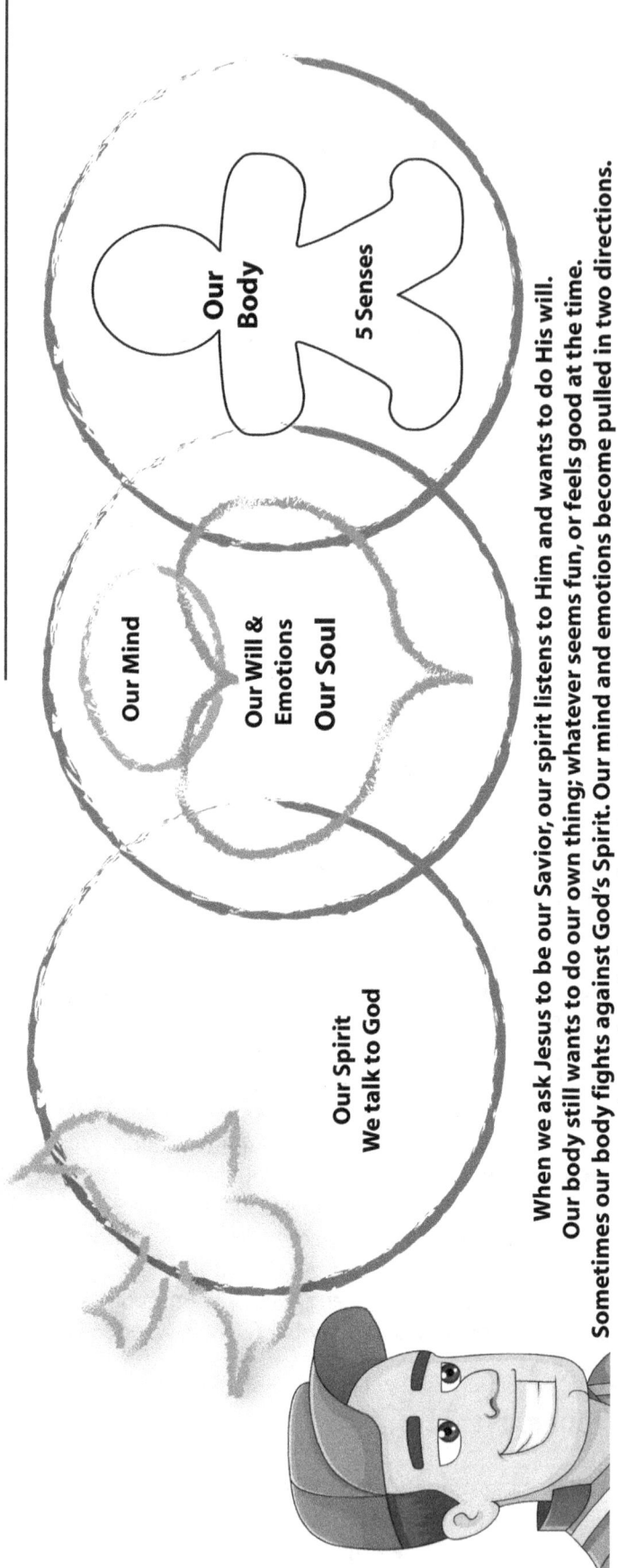

Our Body

5 Senses

Our Mind

Our Will & Emotions

Our Soul

Our Spirit
We talk to God

When we ask Jesus to be our Savior, our spirit listens to Him and wants to do His will.
Our body still wants to do our own thing; whatever seems fun, or feels good at the time.
Sometimes our body fights against God's Spirit. Our mind and emotions become pulled in two directions.
Be wise and seek the Lord and you will find the peace that lasts and lasts.

IDENTITY AND DESTINY
AMAZING KIDS *FOR*

Lesson 15

Memory Verse: **John 8:32**
"Then you will know the truth, and the truth will set you free."

Objective: To Find Out What's Stopping You

⇨ **IDENTIFYING THE LIES AND THEIR CAUSE**

Coach Tom and Coach Pam continued to teach the campers about False Evidence Appearing Real and the effects of the spiritual battle that rages around and in every person. Coach Tom held up a large bungee cord for everyone to see. "Anyone know what this is?" He asked the group. "Several campers answered, "A bungee cord," "A tie down strap," "An elastic band," "A jumper's cord."
"All very good answers," Coach Tom nodded. Let's take a look at how this works. He asked for a couple of volunteers to step forward and he wrapped the stretchy cord around the waist of the first camper. The second camper was an older boy and much bigger than the first. The older boy was given the ends of the cord to hold onto. Coach Tom challenged the younger boy, "Now that the cord is secure around your waist I want you to run toward those trees over there." Coach Tom pointed to a grove of trees several yards away. The boy began to pull and run but the bigger boy held tightly to the ends of the cord. The younger camper ran in place and pulled with all of his might, but he went nowhere.
"Very nicely done!" Coach Tom gave both boys a pat on the back as they sat back down with the others.
"Tell me about what we just saw here," he asked the group. Brodie raised his hand, "The younger boy was too small to overcome the resistance of the older and stronger boy, so he ran until he was worn out, but he got nowhere." "Great answer!" Coach Tom agreed. I want you to remember this example whenever you encounter limiting beliefs about yourself, your abilities and your circumstances."

MOSAIC PIECE

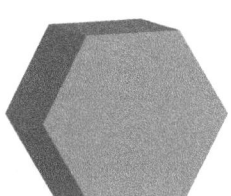

LIMITING BELIEF:
Negative thoughts, deep in our subconscious that keep us from seeing the truth.

Coach Pam shared, "A limiting belief is a deep, hidden belief that you hold. It's a way of seeing yourself that is so ingrained that you don't even realize it's there. The bungee cord in our demonstration limited the ability of the smaller boy to move ahead. It represented the way our beliefs limit our ability to move ahead in life. When those deep beliefs are rooted in F.E.A.R. then the result is what we simply call a LIE!

Resistance is OPPOSITION

Let's look at this from two perspectives. When you are trying to accomplish something that you should do, want to do, or MUST do; opposition can prevent you from achieving your goal.
A football game is a good example of this. The offense wants to get the ball into the end zone to score a touchdown. The defense is trying to prevent them from scoring, creating **Opposing Resistance."**

Form two teams, mark a "territory" for each team and give them several balloons of one color. Each team has its own color such as the blue team and the red team. Challenge the class to try to get all of their balloons into the other team's territory while defending their space from the other team's balloons. Allow several minutes to play the game. Count the number of each color balloons on each side. The team with the fewest balloons in their zone is the winning team.

Consider this; another definition for resistance is, the ability to resist as in the body's resistance to disease.

This is the kind of opposition we need in order to follow through with the Bible verse that says, "Submit to God, resist the devil and he will flee from you." Think about it like this: You are a 2nd grade girl and a 5th grade girl is bullying you; stepping on your feet in line, knocking your books on the floor, saying mean things to you. You have a big brother. He and his friends play basketball and are very popular at the school. What would happen if your brother found out that this girl was picking on you and he and his friends invited you to hang out with them at recess? Do you think the girl will bother you now?

This is how it works when the devil messes with you. He knows he can take you - pick on you and bully you. When you ask Jesus for help, He is your big brother who backs you up and chases the devil away. Satan is no match for Jesus. Next time you're in a fix and need help, ask Jesus to back you up. He cares even more than any other big brother ever could.

YOUR LIMITING BELIEFS

Let's spread out around the room and give yourself plenty of room. We're going to quietly consider some of the limiting beliefs that many people hold onto. Let's apply the light of God's truth to our limiting beliefs.
(Ask the students to turn to journal page 15 and give the class some time to work quietly on their answers.)

Offer several examples of limiting beliefs that are common with children. **"I'm not good enough because I can't play sports."** Then offer the **TRUTH** statement from the Bible that reveals what God has to say about that limiting belief. **1 Cor. 12:12 Our bodies have many parts, and God has put each part just where He wants it."**
"I'm not smart enough."
Proverbs 2:6 For the Lord grants wisdom. From his mouth come knowledge and understanding.

"I never get what I want."

Matthew 6:25-33 "Your heavenly Father already knows all your needs. Seek the Kingdom of God above all else, and live righteously, and he will give you everything you need."

When you apply the truth of God's Word to your thoughts, you'll find that the emphasis in our mind is often placed in the wrong things. We need to see life the way God sees it. Then we will be wise and understand how to live successful, fulfilled lives. (Student's might need help finding the Bible truth statement that fits their limiting belief. Recruit some helpers to work with the students as they search for the answers to their limiting beliefs. This exercise will teach children how to search for answers to their problems in the Word of God.)

RUBBER BAND RESISTANCE

Stack 6 plastic cups in a pyramid on a table about 6 feet from the players. Use masking tape to mark a line on the floor where players should stand. Give the players a bowl full of rubber bands. Use the rubber bands as missiles to shoot down the stack of cups. This game can be played as teams try to see who can knock their stack down first. When the first player in line dismantles the stack of cups, quickly reassemble it and let the next player shoot at it. The first team to successfully knock down the cups once per each player is the winning team.

What does this game teach us?
Satan tries to put obstacles in our way to keep us from God's truth. He uses wrong thinking and limiting beliefs as some of his tools to create walls to keep us from fulfilling our potential. The next time you have negative or limiting thoughts enter your mind, imagine yourself shooting them down with truth statements just like these rubber bands can shoot down the obstacles in this game.

Pray for the students: "Dear Lord, Please help these children to remember Your truth about them. When limiting beliefs attack their thoughts, help them to remember to use the Word of God, which is the Sword of the Spirit, to fight back. Replace every negative thought in their minds with the Truth that sets them free."

IDENTITY AND DESTINY

AMAZING KIDS FOR

Lesson 15

NAME: _____ DATE: _____

MEMORY VERSE: John 8:32 "Then you will know the truth, and the truth will set you free." *Write the verse here.*
Memorize it at home.

Objective: What's Stopping You?

MOSAIC PIECE
LIMITING BELIEF: Negative thoughts, deep in our subconscious that keep us from seeing the truth.

CAPTURE IT! - F.E.A.R.
False Evidence Appearing Real
When something is false – it's a LIE! Don't fall for it. Know God's Word – it's the TRUTH and it will set you free.

Let's look at the at some thoughts that need to be replaced in your mind. Look at the two part equation for each of the LIES that you have allowed yourself to believe. Then fill in the TRUE statement that will replace the lie.

The Lie: _____

What caused you to believe this?

Limiting Belief: _____

What limiting belief resulted from the lie?

God's Truth: _____

_____
My New Empowering Belief

The Lie: _____

What caused you to believe this?

Limiting Belief: _____

What limiting belief resulted from the lie?

God's Truth: _____

_____
My New Empowering Belief

For every limiting belief you have held, you have a promise in God's Word that will replace it. It's important to learn that verse and make it one of your personal memory verses. Everytime the negative thought, or limiting belief pops in your head; immediately combat it with the truth from God's Word that will empower you to fulfill all of the plans God has for you.

IDENTITY AND DESTINY
AMAZING KIDS *FOR*

Lesson 16

Memory Verse: **PSALM 145:18**
"The Lord is near to all who call on Him, to all who call on Him in truth."

Objective: To Find Out What's Stopping You

⇨ **SAFELY OVER THE BRIDGE**

Many of the campers experienced deep and heartfelt relief after finishing the exercise revealing the lies they had accepted as true. Some shed tears and others were joyful. Everyone was glad to have truth statements from the Bible to hold onto.
Coach Pam explained, "You may find the old beliefs and negative thoughts creeping in again after you have replaced them with TRUE BELIEFS. That is normal and it just shows that you need to keep memorizing and rehearsing your new beliefs until they become so much a part of your thinking that they can't be shaken. God wants you to know His truth and He will help you so trust Him, pray and memorize your truth statements every day."

"We are about to move on to the next phase of our adventure." Coach Tom instructed. "Everyone has done a great job so far, and I want to give you the most important piece of your mosaic now." The campers stirred with excitement and a buzzing sound, like bees seemed to fly around them as they wondered what this piece might be. "Before you move on to your final phase of I & D Camp, we want to start the final action step with a Prayer of Commitment. We know that you want to make a difference in the world and live a life that counts. In order to do that you must make sure that the path is clear and your heart is ready. When you pray the prayer on your journal page today, we ask you to be thoughtful and fearless to achieve all that the Lord has for you, you must surrender and submit to God."

MOSAIC PIECE

COMMITMENT:
A PROMISE THAT GUIDES YOUR BEHAVIOR.

(Turn to journal page 16 and ask the students to do the same in their workkbooks. Pray the prayer of Commitment with them.)

Coach Pam added, "As you pray this prayer, we want you to understand that letting go and letting God direct your life can be scary. You fight with wanting to stay in control; make your own decisions, do your own thing." "Always remember," Coach Tom continued, "Even though it may seem hard sometimes, trusting God with your life and your decisions is the only way to live your Identity and Destiny." Coach Tom directed the campers to follow him as he continued to speak, "A prayer of commitment to God is a bit like this zip line," he pointed toward a platform that was about six feet off of the ground. Above it was a long wire that stretched over a lake that the campers often enjoyed. "As you accept God's power in your life, you yield to His wisdom and guidance, trusting Him to see you safely over the obstacles." Coach Tom continued to direct the attention of the campers toward the platform as one of the counselors strapped on a safety harness and grasped the handle of the zip line. "When you say 'Amen" to God's power in your life, you let go of your own power," The counselor lifted his feet from the platform and swooshed above the lake on the zip line. "You are fully trusting God's power and His direction." The campers cheered as the counselor landed safely on the other side of the lake. "Now, who wants to go first?"

ZIP LINE FAITH

Have you ever felt the excitement and thrill of zipping through the air over a large space with nothing but a handbar on a long cord?

(To demonstrate you can show a video clip of some zip line activities from the Internet. Even better; if you have the ability, take the class on a field trip to a ropes course in your area and let them experience the thrill of flying through the air.)

Imagine the feeling of the wind whistling past you, the feeling of flight, and even the thrill of feeling like the zip line has control over the situation, but you are completely at it's mercy.

Now imagine the feeling of grasping the bar, lifting your feet with a push, and soaring! That lift is the feeling that comes when you let go of the control in your life and trust God to lead you in His direction. How can you be sure that you are hearing God and trusting the right voice?

BY SPENDING TIME
READING THE BIBLE - HIS MESSAGE
LISTENING FOR HIS DIRECTIONS IN PRAYER
DEVELOPING YOUR RELATIONSHIP WITH GOD

How do you develop a friendship with a neighbor or classmate?

What are some of the things you do?

In the same way, you must spend time to develop your relationship with God. You need to get to know what He likes and what He doesn't like so that you can tell when something makes Him happy or sad.

When you know what God likes, what He doesn't like, what He sounds like and how He speaks; you can be sure that He does talk to you and give you direction.

HEARING GOD'S VOICE

How do you know for sure that you are hearing God's voice? Check out the three steps that follow:

1 PREPARATION - Am I ready?

Are you spending time with the Lord? Like everything else, developing a hearing ear takes practice.

2 LISTENING - Am I willing?

Sometimes we think that spending time with God means we do all the talking. We need to practice quietly listening - Psalm 46:10 "Be still and know that I am God."

3 CONFIRMATION - Am I sure?

God's word is the litmus test for everything that He says. If you can find two or three Scriptures that clearly agree with what you believe the Lord is saying to you, then you can be sure it is true and it is His word for you.

OBJECT LESSON - LITMUS TEST

Demonstrate for the class the use of litmus paper with a base and an acid. Use baking soda in water for the base element, and vinegar or lemon juice for the acid. When you dip the test strip into the liquid it will turn either pink or blue clearly showing the type of element.

The Bible is the litmus test for determining whether a thought or feeling is truly God's will. He never contradicts His Word.

A.S.K.

When you begin to practice hearing God's voice remember what He said in Matthew 7:7.

A - Ask and it will be given,

S - Seek and you will find,

K - Knock and the door will be opened.

ACTIVE LEARNING - The Candy Zip Line

If you don't have access to a real zip line, create a mini one using a straw, some M & M candies without peanuts, a bowl to hold candies and a bowl to drop the candies into. Form 2 teams and in relay fashion, each player must use their straw to suction and hold a candy as they walk across the playing area to a table with a bowl (at least 10 -15 feet away.) Hold the candy using only the suction from your straw, deliver the candy safely to the other bowl and drop the candy into the bowl. Repeat until the objective is accomplished. The next player on the team then tries to do the same. The first team with all players across wins.

KEEP IT UP

Using only your breath, keep a feather aloft for 60 seconds. This demonstrates how the Holy Spirit works - we don't see Him but we see His effects in our lives.

IDENTITY AND DESTINY
AMAZING KIDS FOR

Lesson 16

NAME: _____ DATE: _____

MEMORY VERSE: Psalm 145:18

"The Lord is near to all who call on Him, to all who call on Him in truth."

Write the verse here.

Objective: What's Stopping You?

Memorize it at home.

MOSAIC PIECE
COMMITMENT: A promise that guides your behavior.

CAPTURE IT! "Let go and let God." It's a common phrase, but it's much easier said than done. As we pray this prayer of commitment today, let's submit our will to God.

Wrapping it Up

In the Bible, the Lord often had the Israelites place stones as a memorial when they accomplished something big. The stone was a reminder to them so that they would remember God's promises. (See Joshua 4:7 for example.) In the same way, our mosaic stones are reminders to us of the work God is doing in our lives. When we put them all together, we will have a beautiful picture of the person God has created us to be.

Our prayer of Commitment represents a very important moment between you and God. It is an important part of your mosaic.

Dear Lord,

I come to You, praising You and thanking You as my Creator. You are mighty, powerful, holy and in charge.

I humbly seek You, asking forgiveness for any sin in my life and I ask you to show me the sins I don't know about. Cleanse me, oh Lord and guide me in Your righteousness.

Today, I offer myself to you. I pray that You will help me see and know my purpose, that You will guide me and use me according to my Identity, Destiny, and the Assignments that You have for my life.

Whenever my stubborn self-will gets in the way, please set me free.

Take away any obstacles that keep me from the purpose You have for my life.

I pray that living my life according to Your purpose will produce the results that You desire and bear witness to Your power, love, and glory.

Having given much thought to this prayer, I am ready.

Help me to finally let go of my will and completely trust You.

May I do Your will always.

Love,

IDENTITY AND DESTINY
AMAGING KIDS  FOR
Lesson 17

Memory Verse: **John 10:3-4**
"He calls His own sheep by name and leads them out, and His sheep follow Him because they know His voice."

Objective: Hearing God's Voice

⇨ **In a Quiet Place**

One by one the campers strapped on a harness, a helmet, and put on sturdy gloves. Each learned how to control the handle on the zip line to either speed up, slow down or stop. Several campers shouted and some screamed as they swooped across the lake and over to the opposite shore. Chris thought this was a great way to travel and wished he had one that could take him anywhere he needed to go. Zoé laughed with glee as she soared over the lake. She looked to the sky and saw Perry soaring above her. Her faithful falcon was seldom far from her side. Zoé imagined that she was flying like Perry and she had a new appreciation for her pet as she felt the wind rush past her. Grace was afraid of the zip line. She didn't trust the harness or the steel cable. Coach Tom assured her she would be quite safe and so she finally consented to strap herself in and take her turn. She hesitated as she prepared her launch. She thought about turning back. The longer she hesitated, the more scared she became. Suddenly, she felt a push from behind. Reese was there to "encourage" her along, "Come on Grace, you can do it!" She shouted as she gave a firm push. "AAAAIIIIEEEEE!"
Grace screamed as she lifted off the platform and swept over the lake. She was past the point of turning back and decided she enjoyed the ride after all. "I'm going to get that Reese," she thought, but she smiled all the same.
The campers laughed and talked excitedly about their experience. They cheered as each new arrival landed safely on the far side of the lake.

MOSAIC PIECE

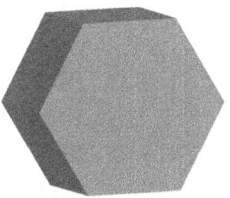

MEDITATION:
THINKING QUIETLY AND DEEPLY

As the last campers gathered, Coach Tom congratulated them, "Well done, everyone. Now we have a special treat for you. Follow me." Coach Tom led the campers to a beautiful garden. It was filled with flowers, trees and hedges. Several sculptures, art objects and fountains dotted the garden. A soft breeze blew the fragrance of delicate flowers through the air and the campers breathed deeply to enjoy the aroma. The laughter and talk among the campers softened as they wondered about this new experience. The place alone was enough to calm them from their recent flight across the lake.

Coach Pam was there in the garden. She greeted the campers, "Welcome everyone to our meditation gardens." She smiled as she continued, "This is one of my favorite places in the entire camp." The campers could understand why as they took in the atmosphere around them. Coach Tom added, "We are going to enjoy this garden for the next 30 minutes as we teach you how to quiet yourself and listen for God's voice. When we tell you to begin, we will ask you to find a spot here in the garden. We want you to spread out and give each other plenty of space. This is a personal time so we ask you to not talk to your neighbor until we leave the garden. We have also supplied journal pages and pencils for you to write your thoughts and feelings as you rest quietly."
"Okay everybody, let's get settled," Coach Pam encouraged the campers and they each took a pencil and a journal page as they moved quietly around the garden finding their perfect spot.

QUIET TIME WITH GOD

Jesus often spent quiet time alone with God. He would find a place on a mountain or in a peaceful garden and pray. He asked God for wisdom but best of all, He spent time just being with God.

How do you feel when you get to spend time with a best friend? It's exciting and fun because you do things together that you both enjoy. That's what God wants in His relationship with you. Today we are going to take some time in a quiet place to listen for God and hear what He wants to say to us.

Use a prayer room or a garden if one is available for this excercise and be sure to work with groups small enough so that everyone has plenty of alone space. You can create the space in a classroom using fragrant candles or wall plug-in fragrance, soft music, and dim lights. Give each student a journal page and a pencil. Encourage the class to relax and silence their thoughts. Invite them to ask the Three Amigos; the critical, skeptical and judgmental parts of their thoughts to leave the room. Picture them going out the door and shutting it behind them.

Invite the students to imagine themselves in a peaceful garden just like in our story. Smell the flowers in the air, feel the soft warm breeze, hear the birds chirping in the trees. Now imagine that Jesus is with you in the garden. Enjoy the sights and smells of the garden with Him.

Now ask Jesus if you can speak with Him today. What does He say?

Next ask HIm one of the questions on your journal page. 1 Jesus, what is my identity, who am I?

Write down the thoughts and feelings that come to mind. Pause and just listen. What do you hear? What are you thinking about now? Write it down. Continue with each of your questions. When you are finished, thank Jesus for speaking with you. Let Him know how much you love Him. Remember, He wants to be your best friend. As you finish the exercise, picture the Three Amigos coming back into the room. Finally, gather your things and prepare to leave the quiet place. Do you have any more thoughts you'd like to share with Jesus? He loves to hear what you think.

CAN YOU HEAR GOD SPEAKING?

2 Chronicles 7:14

Allow the class to make crosses using chenille wires, popsicle sticks or paper pieces glued to a paper cross in mosaic fashion. Read the Bible passage as the students work on their project. As they create their crafts ask them to be willing to be the people that the Bible speaks about; those who will be humble, pray, seek God, and obey Him. Notice that each of the four sides of the cross corresponds to one of the four statements in this passage.

If the cross is on paper or popsicle sticks, ask the class to write one of the four commands on each side of the cross.

⇨   ACTIVE LEARNING

The Bible compares Jesus to a Good Shepherd, and His people are like sheep. It says that if even one goes missing, He will leave the 99 in the pen and search for the lost sheep.

Sheep tend to be very curious. They will get out of their pen and wander into trouble. That's why the shepherd has to hunt for them. They must stay in the pen to keep them safe from deep water, poisonous weeds, and hungry predators.

We're going to play a game that helps us understand how Jesus searches for us and looks after us. Select a player to be the shepherd. Use masking tape to make a circle on the floor that is large enough to contain all of the remaining students or "sheep." (If you have an outdoor area you can use chalk to draw a circle on the pavement.)

The shepherd hides his eyes and counts to 10 while all of the sheep scatter and hide. If the shepherd catches or sees you, you must go to the circle or "pen." When the shepherd goes to search for other sheep, those in the pen begin to bleat like sheep, "Baa, baa!" If one of the other sheep who is still hiding returns your signal, you run and hide again while the shepherd isn't looking. If the shepherd catches or sees you trying to run away, you must return to the pen. When all of the sheep are safely in the pen, the game is over and another player is selected to be the shepherd.

IDENTITY AND DESTINY
AMAZING KIDS  FOR

Lesson 17

NAME: _____ DATE: _____

MEMORY VERSE: John 10:3-4 "He calls His own sheep by name and leads them out, and His sheep follow Him because they know His voice."

Write the verse here.
Memorize it at home.

_____

_____

_____

MOSAIC PIECE
MEDITATION:
THINKING QUIETLY AND DEEPLY

CAPTURE IT! Take time to hear God speak to you. You can practice at home. Be very still and ask Him a question. Wait for the answer. Write it down. Thank Him for talking to you.

Objective: Hearing God's Voice

Be very still as you prepare to hear God speak to you. Take a few deep breaths to calm yourself. Ask God some questions:

1. Lord, may I speak with you today? _____

2. Lord, what is my identity? Who am I? _____

3. Lord, what do you want me to do when I grow up? _____

4. Do you have a special task for me Lord? _____

Write any words, thoughts or feelings that come to your mind, even if they don't make sense to you.

_____

Ask God to help you understand anything that you didn't understand. Ask Him, "Can You explain that more?" If you want to draw a picture about your quiet time with God you may use a blank page at the back of your journal. Write Lesson 17 on your picture.

IDENTITY AND DESTINY
AMAZING KIDS FOR

Lesson 18

Memory Verse: **Daniel 2:19**
"During the night the mystery was revealed to Daniel in a dream."

Objective: Hearing God's Voice

⇨ **Was It All a Dream?**

As the campers finished their quiet time in the garden they felt calm and peaceful. Even the most energetic campers had a softer and quieter way of speaking to one another. Coach Pam gathered the campers together in a group, "I'm so proud of the great work you've done here today campers." She congratulated the group as they sat down on the grass around her. "I want you to remember this exercise and practice regularly at home. It will give you strength for your life, and direction from the Lord."

Coach Pam added, "I'd like to tell you about another form of meditation that you can take with you anywhere you go." As she spoke, she held out the palm of her hand so that everyone could see. A sticky note with a verse was stuck to her hand. "Even grown-ups need to memorize verses from Scripture and think deeply about the meaning of the words."

Coach Pam continued, "A dear friend of mine taught me his way of meditating on the Bible and I want to share it with you. When you get up in the morning, give yourself extra time to read your Bible. Pick out a verse that particularly strikes you that day. Write it on a sticky note and carry it with you all day. Pull it out and read it now and then. Think about each word. Ask the Lord to explain it to you. Is there a specific message that He wants you to get from this verse? When you go to school you can think about it. When you are at recess or in the gym, think about the verse over and over. When you get specific ideas about the verse, write them down.

This is what I call my **Manna for the Day.** It's about hiding God's Word in my heart. You are learning to have a conversation with God and He is teaching you new things every day."

MOSAIC PIECE

DREAM:
1. THOUGHTS OR IMAGES WHILE ASLEEP. 2. A STRONGLY DESIRED GOAL OR VISION.

Coach Tom added, "Another way that God speaks to us is in dreams. There are several examples in the Bible of people who experienced dreams that gave them God's wisdom. Think about Jacob and the ladder that he saw. It had angels walking up and down it and it stretched all the way to heaven. Joseph, son of Jacob had dreams. Daniel recorded dreams in Scripture. Another Joseph was instructed in a dream to marry his wife Mary, the mother of Jesus. He learned that God gave her the baby she carried. In another dream, he felt he must move his family away from Israel because as long as King Herod was alive, Jesus was not safe. Can you think of some other Bible examples, or maybe some examples in your own life of dreams that spoke strongly to you?" Several campers shared examples and Coach Tom encouraged them, "Very good! Now how do you prepare yourself to hear from God in your sleep?" You can't guarantee that every dream you have will be from God but when you go to bed at night, think about the challenges of your day. Relax, let any of the stress from the day roll off of you. Ask the Lord to carry the burden for you. Ask the Lord to speak to you and give you purpose-filled dreams. Keep a journal and pen by your bed. When you wake up, write down any thoughts, images or feelings that you have. Don't worry if it makes sense or not. Some of your dreams will be from God and some will not. How do you know the difference? Ask Him to show you Scripture that lines up with the dream, or ask for confirmation through someone you trust.

That night, all the campers had pens and notepads by their bunks. Chris was so tired from all of the things he had experienced that he doubted whether he would remember anything but he prayed as he went to sleep, "Lord, please help me to remember all that I've learned in the last couple of days. Help me to hear You as I sleep, and help me to understand what You want to say to me." Chris sighed and rested his head on his pillow. Bernie curled up right beside his bed. He was sound asleep in minutes and smiled as he dreamed about the exciting and very unexpected camp experience.

Chris felt Bernie's cold, wet nose on his face. "What time is it? What's wrong boy? " He groaned, and turned his head to the side to face Bernie, the back of his head was sore." He touched it and realized he had a bump on the back of his head. "Oww! How did I do that?" Chris was puzzled, "Am I dreaming?" He wondered. Next he heard Zoé's voice, "Chris, are you okay? Wake up! Wake up!" She seemed worried. Suddenly he felt cold and wet instead of warm and cozy in his bunk. "What's going on?" He wondered. "Chris! Oh thank God! I was afraid I wouldn't be able to wake you!" Zoé seemed afraid, and Chris slowly opened his eyes and focused on her face. Her hair was wet and hanging in her face. She had tears streaming down her cheeks and her clothes were drenched. Chris realized that he was not in his bunk at camp. He was lying on the ground in the rain at the foot of the tree house in Zoé's woods. Soon Chris heard the familiar, "Caw, caw," of Perry's cry. Zoé called out, "Over here!" Suddenly two of her brothers ran up to her and Chris. They were worried too. Chris was still trying to figure out what had happened as the boys made sure he was okay, "No broken bones, probably a concussion," they seemed 100 miles away as they touched his arms and legs and looked into his eyes. The boys gently lifted him and began to carry him to the big farm house where Zoé lived with her family.

Chris was beginning to remember what happened. He must have hit his head pretty hard when he slipped from the steps of the tree house. He was in such a hurry to get out of the storm that he lost his footing.

Was all of this only a dream? Did he really go to Camp I & D? He was so sure about the things he learned and the people that he met; and yet he wondered if it had happened at all. As he was beginning to regain his focus, he reached into his pocket. There he felt several stones. He pulled one out, sure enough, it was a beautiful, shiny stone that he had saved from the campfire after his night in the woods. "Wow! It wasn't a dream! Or was it?" He had quite a story to tell Zoé as he rested and recovered from his fall.

CAN YOU HEAR GOD SPEAKING?

Practice at home the discipline of hearing God in your dreams. When you wake up in the morning, write down what you dreamed about. You should ask God what your dream means and if He is speaking to you in the dream.

Not every dream is from God. As you practice writing them down, you will also get better at understanding them.

⇨ **ACTIVE LEARNING - STICKY VERSES**

Supply sticky notes, colorful pens, pencils and mini stickers. Ask the students to recall one of their favorite verses from previous lessons, or choose the verse from today's lesson. Invite them to write the verse on their sticky note and decorate it with designs. Let them use their imagination and get creative with their notes.

Remind the class of the exercise that Coach Pam described.
Where can you put your sticky note so that you will see it several times throughout the day?
Place your sticky there and everytime you see it say the verse out loud. Before you know it, that verse will stick in your mind. Be sure to ask God questions about the verse.
"How does this verse apply to me?"
"What do You want me to learn from this verse?"
"How can I apply this verse to my life?"

As you learn to talk to God about the Word, and listen for His answers, you are growing in the discipline of being a "Doer of the Word."

IDENTITY AND DESTINY

AMAZING KIDS FOR

Lesson 18

NAME: _____ DATE: _____

MEMORY VERSE: Daniel 2:19 "During the night the mystery was revealed to Daniel in a dream."

Write the verse here.
Memorize it at home.

Objective: Hearing God's Voice

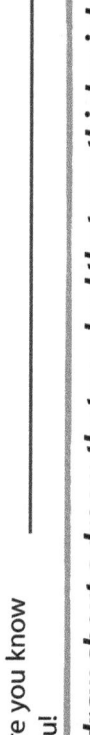

Practice writing your favorite verses on sticky notes. Put them in a place where you will see them often. Say them out loud everytime you see them. Before you know it, your verses will stick with you!

"I know the plans I have for you," says the Lord. Jer. 29:11

MOSAIC PIECE

DREAM: 1. THOUGHTS OR IMAGES WHILE ASLEEP. 2. A STRONGLY DESIRED GOAL OR VISION.

CAPTURE IT!

Many people in the Bible experienced dreams that gave them God's wisdom. Think about Jacob and the ladder that he saw. It had angels walking up and down and it stretched all the way to heaven. Joseph, son of Jacob had dreams. Daniel recorded dreams in Scripture. Another Joseph was told in a dream to marry his wife Mary.

Write or draw about a dream that you had that you think might be from God.

IDENTITY AND DESTINY AMAZING KIDS FOR

Lesson 19

Memory Verse: **Matthew 7:7**
"Keep on asking, and you will receive what you ask for. Keep on seeking, and you will find. Keep on knocking, and the door will be opened to you."

Objective: Crystallize Your Purpose Statement

➪ **WHO AM I AND WHY AM I HERE?**

Have you ever been on a road trip that seemed to go on and on? Maybe you asked, "Are we there yet?" This adventure with Chris and Zoé has been like that. What do parents usually say when you ask that question? "We're almost there!"

We are in the final step of assembling the pieces of our purpose mosaic and revealing the masterpiece that God designed when He created you.
When we put all of the pieces together, you will be able to answer the questions, "Who am I?" And, "Why am I here?" You will also be able to identify some of the assignments that God has for you. Look for short-term tasks and projects that fit you, not just the big goals of "what you want to be when you grow up," but some here and now steps to help you grow spiritually, as well as mentally. School is one of your primary assignments now. Can you think of some other tasks that you do now that help prepare you for your future?

As we assemble our mosaic, we will look back at all of our previous lessons to remember what we learned along the way. Our results will all be written together in a final step that will remain as a great reminder as you step toward your future.

Remember:
You do the steps and God does the rest!

MOSAIC PIECE

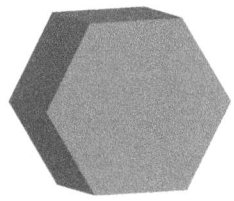

MOSAIC:

A surface decoration made by inlaying small pieces of variously colored material to form pictures or patterns.

WHAT A GIFT!
Why do we call your identity, destiny and purpose statements a mosaic?
Just like a mosaic, you are putting together several pieces of information that tell something about you. When you put them all together you see a bigger picture - that is, God's unique design that makes you who you are.
You have learned a lot about yourself and your unique qualities by this time. Just think about the benefits to your life when you approach your choices for your future in the light of your mosaic.
In the final part in this process, you hold in your hand a reference tool that you can look back at often, continue to use the lessons and the journal pages as you get older. Continue journaling your prayer times with the Lord and memorizing Scripture. Continue capturing your dreams in your journal to see how God might speak to you in them. The skills that you have learned in Identity and Destiny will help you stay on track toward your Purpose for the rest of your life!

Remember above all, no matter how busy you are, God is most interested in your relationship with Him. Our number one purpose is to abide, remain in Him, listen to Him, and obey Him.

THE REST OF THE STORY

Take a moment and think about the beginning of our adventure with Chris and Zoé. When Chris arrived at Zoé's house, he was excited to add his shiny piece of blue glass to the collection of rocks and other treasures that lined a wall in the treehouse.

Throughout the entire story Chris added stones to his pocket every time he had a unique and memorable experience. In the Bible, God instructed the Israelites to do this too. When they experienced His miracle power, He told them to set up some stones, or build an altar of stone in order to remember what He did for them. Everytime someone passed by the place of the miracle, they would see these stones and remember God's love and provision for them.

In the story we shared, Chris collected stones because he was in the habit of doing it. The interesting point at the end of the story is that Chris is not sure if his fall from the tree and a bump on his head caused him to dream the whole adventure, or had he really been in all of those places? Were Coach Tom, Coach Pam and his new friends real; or was it all just a dream? If it was just a dream, does it make the things he learned any less valid or important?

We also learn in the Bible that God was able to teach people His wisdom, or give them direction in dreams. When Chris was fully awake at the foot of the treehouse, he reached into his pocket. What he found there was a shiny, black stone that he put in his pocket from the fire that he helped build during his night in the woods with his friends. Now what was he to think? The stone made his adventure more real, and yet, here he was back in his own neighborhood. The story leaves you wondering about all of the possibilities, as well as the seeming impossibilities. Either way, Chris learned a lot of valuable lessons.

What would you do next if you were Chris?
Do you think Zoé might remember the adventures too if they really did happen?
Use your imagination and decide what happens next. Finish the story on your journal page.

WHAT'S YOUR STORY?

Supply 11X17 paper or cardstock for each student. Collect colorful pens, pencils, stickers, magazines and various art supplies.
Ask the students to think about their life. Think about their family, hobbies, likes and dislikes. Ask them to recall their gifts, identity, core values, and desires for their future. (Ask them to refer back to the results from previous lessons to complete the task.)

Create a story board using the items provided.
Ask questions about the pictures and ideas that the students choose.
"How does this picture apply to me?" "What does it represent?" "How does this tell your story?"

The students can use pictures and writing boxes, words, pictures, colors all say something about us.
If you were to create your story around a single item; like Chris and his rock collection, what would that item be? How does it explain your story?

Once the students complete their story board, ask them to explain it.
* You might want to take a picture of it and add it to their assessments and journal pages from the lessons.
**Create your own story board to give an example of what it should look like.

MY MOSAIC

Each student should have a copy of the book that is now complete. The assessments and the lessons are valuable tools for future reference. Encourage the students to review their results again in the future. When they are in their mid-teens they should review these concepts again by taking the course written for adults, "Identity and Destiny, Seven Steps to a Purpose Filled Life," by Tom and Pam Wolf.

A final celebration with the students and their parents is great way to celebrate their achievement. Present each student with a certificate of completion and have a party!

IDENTITY AND DESTINY
AMAZING KIDS FOR

Lesson 19

NAME: _____ DATE: _____

MEMORY VERSE: Matthew 7:7 "Keep on asking, and you will receive what you ask for. Keep on seeking, and you will find. Keep on knocking, and the door will be opened to you."

Write the verse here.

Objective: Crystallize Your Purpose Statement

MOSAIC PIECE
MOSAIC: A surface decoration made by inlaying small pieces of variously colored material to form pictures or patterns.

CAPTURE IT! In the Bible, God told the Israelites to set up stones as a reminder when they experienced His miracle power. Chris saved stones like that too. It's like keeping a souvenir of the places you visit. Do you have some special reminders of things that you have done?

What would you do next if you were Chris? Do you think Zoé might remember the adventures too if they really did happen? Use your imagination and decide what happens next. Finish the story here.

Appendix

IDENTITY AND DESTINY
AMAZING KIDS FOR

My Mosaic

NAME: _____ DATE: _____

> "Two roads diverged in a wood, and I took the one less traveled and that has made all of the difference."

Lesson 1

Life is full of choices. God has a plan for you. Jeremiah 29:11

When you listen to God and follow His directions, He helps you fulfill your purpose and His plan for you. His way is always the best way because He already knows how things will turn out in the end.

Will you choose to follow God's plan for your life? _____

Lesson 2

God's purpose is to give you a rich and satisfying life. John 10:10

Your destiny is what you do just by being you. God made you one - of - a kind. When you fulfill your destiny, you are helping others and honoring God.

My Purpose Score _____
You can take action today to improve your purpose score!

Lesson 3

1 Thessalonians 1:4 (TM) It is clear to us, friends, that God not only loves you very much but also has put His hand on you for something special.

IDENTITY It's who I am - not what I do.

Write the totals from each column on your worksheet from the DISC quiz.

Your **D** score is - write it here: _____

Your **I** score is - write it here: _____

Your **S** score is - write it here: _____

Your **C** score is - write it here: _____

In which area do you have the highest number?
Which area is the second highest? _____

These are clues to your personality style. It's a key ingredient to the unique design that God made when He formed you.

Lesson 4

Romans 12:4-5 We are many parts of one body, and we all belong to each other.
ASSIGNMENT: It's what God is asking you to do next.

Your personality makes you specially suited for your assignment.
My DISC Personality is: _____

IDENTITY AND DESTINY
AMAZING KIDS FOR

My Mosaic 2

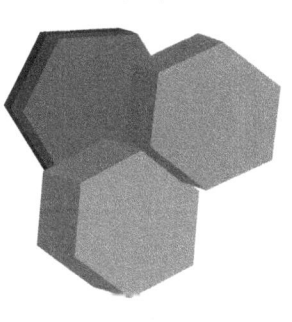

NAME: _____ DATE: _____

Lesson 8 Core Values are like a prism or a filter. They affect the way you view life. If the Bible is your filter, it will help you to fulfill God's purpose for your life.

My Top 5 Core Values

Lesson 9 **SPIRITUAL GIFTS:**

Special abilities given to us by God to equip us to serve others.

My Spiritual Gifts

Lesson 5 & 6

Psalm 139:14 Thank You for making me so wonderfully complex. Your workmanship is marvelous – how well I know it. *BOUNCE BACK!*

RESILIENCE = BOUNCE BACK!

BOING!

HOW BOUNCY ARE YOU?

Highest Resilience Score:

Your ability to bounce back when times are difficulty is affected by 7 different areas. 1 Emotional Self-Control, 2 Impulse Control, 3 Empathy, Identifying with someone else, 4 Optimism, 5 Ability to identify the cause of your problems, 6 Knowing you have an effect on the world, 7 Reaching - Out and taking risks

Lesson 7

1 Corinthians 13:13 "And now these three remain; faith, hope and love. And the greatest of these is love.

CORE VALUES - What matters most to you?

IDENTITY AND DESTINY
AMAZING KIDS  FOR
My Mosaic 3

NAME: _____ DATE: _____

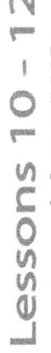

What's your passion?

Lessons 10 – 12
Jeremiah 1:5 TMB

"Before I shaped you in the womb, I knew all about you. Before you saw the light of day, I had holy plans for you."

PASSION PURSUIT:

There is a link between passion and purpose. God has a plan for your life. The things that you feel very strongly about are clues to understanding your purpose.

Discover the Greater Needs: What are some common themes in your passions and the needs that inspire them? What are some words that cause a strong reaction when you think of them?

NEED: Something necessary or desirable.

Lesson 13 ROAD BLOCKS
Isaiah 41:10

"Do not fear, for I am with you, do not be dismayed, for I am your God. I will strengthen you and help you."
What's Stopping You?

STOP

God wants you to be a success!

Our Mind

Our Body

Our Emotions

Our Soul

5 Senses

Our Spirit
We talk to God

Lesson 14 One Person Three Parts

God is Father, Son, and Holy Spirit. We too have 3 distinct and connected parts to our being. We are a spiritual being, with a soul; which is our mind, will and emotions, and we live in a physical body. The body and the spirit want to control our mind which becomes our "battle ground."

When we ask Jesus to be our Savior, our spirit listens to Him and wants to do His will. Our body still wants to do our own thing; whatever seems fun, or feels good at the time. Sometimes our body fights against God's Spirit. Our mind and emotions become pulled in two directions. Be wise and seek the Lord and you will find the peace that lasts and lasts.

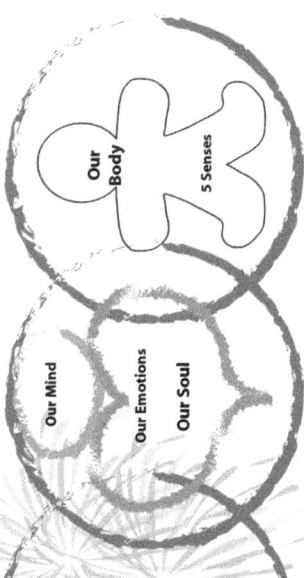

IDENTITY AND DESTINY

AMAZING KIDS 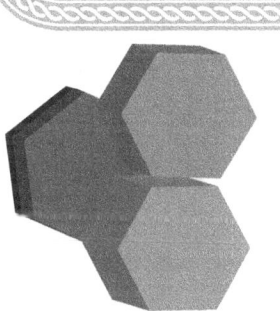 FOR

My Mosaic 4

NAME: _____

Lesson 17   John 10:3-4   "He calls His own sheep by name and leads them out, and His sheep follow Him because they know His voice."   *Hearing God's Voice*

Take time to hear God speak to you.
You can practice at home.
Be very still and ask Him a question.
Wait for the answer. Write it down.

Lesson 15 & 16 John 8:32

"Then you will know the truth, and the truth will set you free."

LIMITING BELIEF: Negative thoughts, deep in our subconscious that keep us from seeing the truth.

F.E.A.R. = False Evidence Appearing Real
When something is false – it's a LIE! Don't fall for it.
Know God's Word – it's the TRUTH and it will set you free.

Lesson 18   DREAMS

Daniel 2:19 "During the night the mystery was revealed to Daniel in a dream."
Hearing God's Voice

Many people in the Bible experienced dreams that gave them God's wisdom. He can speak to you in dreams too.

Write one of your God inspired dreams here.

COMMITMENT: A promise that guides your behavior.

Dear Lord,
I come to You, praising You and thanking You as my Creator. You are mighty, powerful, holy and in charge.
I humbly seek You, asking forgiveness for any sin in my life and I ask you to show me the sins I don't know about. Cleanse me, oh Lord and guide me in Your righteousness.
Today, I offer myself to you. I pray that You will help me see and know my purpose, that You will guide me and use me according to my Identity, Destiny, and the Assignments that You have for my life.
Whenever my stubborn self-will gets in the way, please set me free.
Take away any obstacles that keep me from the purpose You have for my life. I pray that living my life according to Your purpose will produce the results that You desire and bear witness to Your power, love, and glory. Having given much thought to this prayer, I am ready. Help me to finally let go of my will and and completely trust You.
May I do Your will always. Amen.

Notes for Parents Meeting

Living in Purpose on Purpose

What we are called to do.

"Train a child according to his/her God-given bent…" Proverbs 22:6

As children's ministers, counselors, and coaches, we are called to partner with parents to help with the process of training and discovery.

1. Help discover the child's "bent" – Gifts, abilities, personality style.
2. Teach children the Truth – Who is God? How can I be saved? How am I empowered to live a godly life?
3. How do I fulfill God's purpose for my life?

How do I find God's Purpose for Me?

"I know the plans I have for you," says the Lord, "They are plans for good and not disaster, to give you a future and a hope." Jeremiah 29:11

1. Study and memorize Scripture – God's instructions for us.
2. Research personality type, gifts, passions, talents, special qualities, core values, resilience and road blocks.
3. Learn to know God's voice and obey His will.

How do we find God's purpose for us? Study all aspects IQ Intelligence Quotient (20%)+ EQ Emotional Quotient (80%) + "SQ" Spiritual Quotient. How much are we willing to give spiritually to learn God's will, His voice, and obey His plan for us? (He gave 100%)

Your Amazing 3 –Part Being

When we ask Jesus to be our Savior, our spirit listens to Him and wants to do His will.

Our body still wants to do our own thing; whatever seems fun, or feels good at the time.

Sometimes our body fights against God's Spirit. Our mind and emotions become pulled in two directions.

Be wise and seek the Lord and you will find the peace that lasts and lasts.

Your Kingdom Come, Your Will be Done

…"On earth as it is in Heaven…" Matthew 6: 9-13

1. God wants everyone to know Him and be saved.
2. We bring the best witness when we live in our strengths.
3. When we lead in every arena in society, we can influence others with God's righteousness and His kingdom principles.
4. Blessed is the Nation who's God is the Lord.

Developing Leaders in all Areas of Life

When children know their strengths they can begin to set long term goals for their future at a very young age.

1. Helps a young person stay focused.
2. Less prone to peer pressure. "I have a reason to live right, God has a plan for my life."
3. Saves $1000.00's in educational costs and years of searching for the right major.

Lesson 12 page 3

⇨ **REVIEW GAME**

The review game, Purpose in the Pain exercise, and the journal page exercise work well as alternating activities in a "centers" format. Divide the class into 3 groups and allow about 15 minutes for each activity.

Play a bridge crossing game by asking the students review questions. When they answer correctly they may take a step across the bridge. Since there are 3 trolls, or "amigos" you must answer 3 questions correctly to cross safely over the bridge.

Online problem solving games are also available. You might ask a review question and if the student answers correctly, they are permitted to take a turn at the video "Bridge Crossing Game."
You might prefer to set up a "bridge" by roping off an area in the classroom and allowing the students to take turns answering 3 questions. Those who answer all 3 questions correctly cross the bridge and earn a prize.

1. Emotional Regulation "How well you control your emotions" is a good thing to have.
TRUE OR FALSE?
2. In our story about Chris and Zoé, our friends begin an adventure by choosing to take a road that everyone travels.
TRUE OR FALSE?
3. God created you to be unique, or ___1___ of a kind.
4. Optimism means " A positive point of view."
TRUE OR FALSE?
5. In one of our memory verses, Jer. 29:11 we learned that God has a special PLAN for our lives.
6. Destiny is what you __DO__ just by being you.
7. John 10:10 says God's PURPOSE is to give us a rich and satisfying life.
8. In the river crossing, Chris and his friends learned how to work together as a _TEAM_.
9. An assignment is something that you buy at the store.
TRUE OR FALSE?
10. The Action Hero personality, like Leon, is a shy and fearful.
TRUE OR FALSE?
11. Resilience, or "bounce back" is the ability to "splat like an egg" when you hit the floor.
TRUE OR FALSE?

12. Core Values are beliefs that are special to you and that matter the most to you.
TRUE OR FALSE?
13. The Bible says that God is Light. When we allow His love to shine through us, we reflect his light to others.
TRUE OR FALSE?
14. 1 Cor. 13:13 ...The greatest of these is LOVE.
15. Core Values can be compared to a PRISM. They affect the way you view life.
16. Name one of your Core Values. _____
(Answers will vary. See Lesson 8 for examples.)
17. Spiritual gifts are special gifts given by God to every believer.
TRUE OR FALSE?
18. An example of a Spiritual Gift is a new bike for Christmas.
TRUE OR FALSE?
19. 1 Peter 4:10 Each one should use whatever gift he has received to _SERVE_ others.
20. PASSION is a strong, driving feeling or desire.
21. Passion will help you focus on your goals and help you to achieve your purpose.
TRUE OR FALSE?
22. Romans 11:29 "For God's GIFTS and his call can never be withdrawn."
23. Coach Tom and Coach Pam allowed Chris and his friends to get lost on purpose so they would learn a lesson.
TRUE OR FALSE?
24. God doesn't want you to learn about how He designed you because He like to keep things a MYSTERY.
TRUE OR FALSE?
25. In our lesson about the Apostle Paul we learned that there is no guarantee that you will not face obstacles when you are pursuing God's purpose for your life.
TRUE OR FALSE?
26. Discovering your passions, purpose, personality, spiritual gifts, and destiny are compared to gathering pieces of your own personal mosaic.
TRUE OR FALSE?
27. What is a mosaic?
Answers will vary.
Key words: beautiful artwork, stained glass window, unique, art made from several small glass shapes.

About the Author

Libby Hodge holds a doctorate degree in Pastoral Counseling from Chesapeake Bible College and Seminary in Ridgely, MD.

She is also a licensed counselor and member of the American Association of Christian Counselors, and a licensed facilitator with Identity and Destiny.

She has served as a children's minister for over 20 years and has written curriculum for her classes for several years. Libby is also the Children's Ministry Director at Connection Church in Hinesville, GA.

Married to her husband Ed Hodge for 37 years, they have 5 grown children and 4 grandchildren.

Libby has a passion for children and for seeing them grow up to fulfill their purpose in God. She has a gift for motivating and teaching children in ways that are memorable and fun. With a love for learning, and a desire to see kids develop in their God-given gifts and talents, she has embraced the work of interpreting Identity and Destiny, 7 Steps to a Purpose-Filled Life, with joy and a commitment to maintain the integrity of the original work.

Endorsement for Identity and Destiny for Amazing Kids

If you believe that your child benefited from learning about their gifts, strengths and God-given purpose by studying this course, would you be willing to write a statement about how this course helped? Please email your reply to libbyhodge@gmail.com. Thanks! Libby

Name:
Child's Name:
Child's Age   Grade

Did your child benefit from learning about his/her strengths, passions, gifts, resilience personality style, etc?
In what way has this discovery made a difference in your child's perspective?

Has your child become involved in new hobbies, activities or other pursuits since discovering their "sweet spot?" Please describe.

Has your child experienced a more positive outlook on life, learned to overcome certain fears, or develop better "bounce back" when things get tough? Please describe.

Does your child have a stronger sense of purpose, direction or desire concerning what they want to pursue in college or as a career? Please describe.

Has your child developed a stronger sense of God's presence and active involvement in his/her life? Has your child developed a more consistent prayer life or habit of journaling?

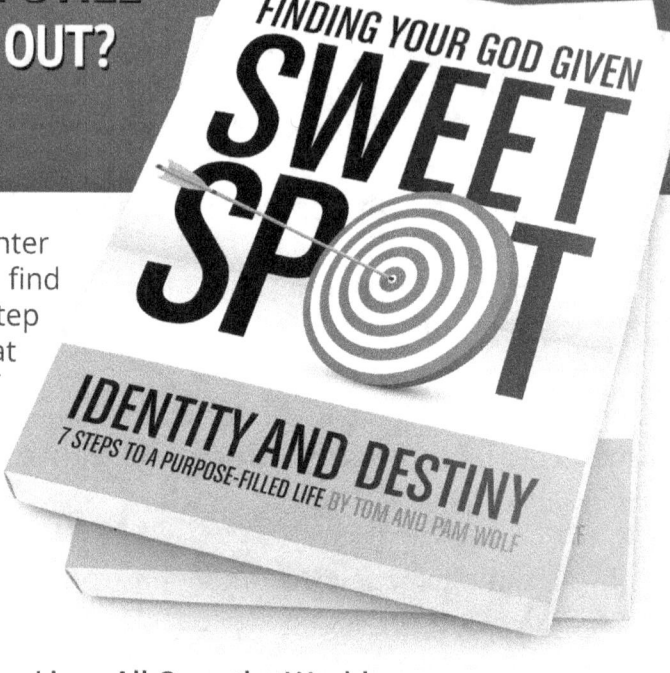

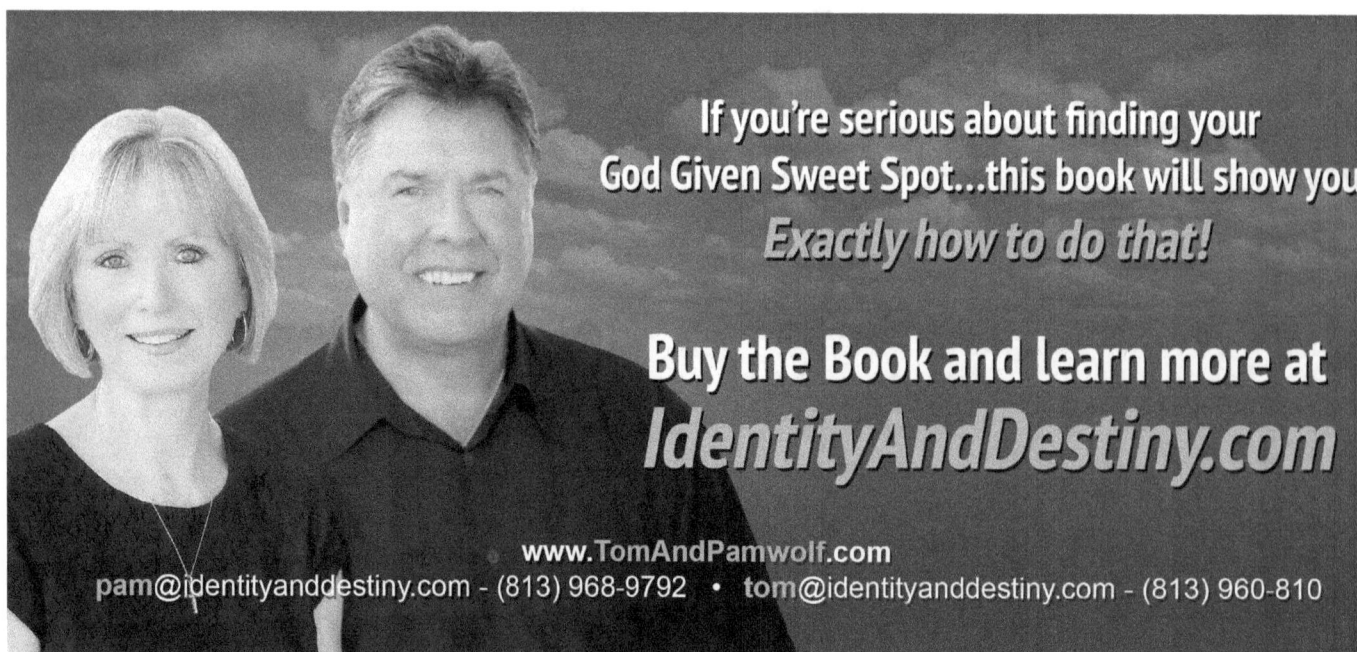

www.ingramcontent.com/pod-product-compliance
Lightning Source LLC
Chambersburg PA
CBHW080316290526
45790CB00005B/2064